city
Secrets

FLORENCE
VENICE

THE ESSENTIAL INSIDER'S GUIDE

ROBERT KAHN

SERIES EDITOR

FANG DUFF KAHN PUBLISHERS

NEW YORK

Fang Duff Kahn Publishers
611 Broadway, floor 4
New York, NY 10012
www.citysecrets.com

2011 2012 2013 2014 / 10 9 8 7 6 5 4 3 2 1

ISBN: 978-0-9835400-0-7

Library of Congress Control Number: 2011929608

Printed in China through Asia Pacific Offset

Distributed by Publishers Group West

Every care has been taken to ensure the accuracy of the information in this book. However, the publisher is not able to accept responsibility for any consequences arising from use of the guide or the information it contains. If you do encounter a factual error, please let us know.

City Secrets books may be purchased at special quantity discounts for business or promotional use. For information, please contact us at info@fangduffkahn.com.

TABLE OF CONTENTS

FLORENCE

Historic Center 10

Oltrarno 20

City Center West 30

City Center North 34

City Center East 42

Colli 45

Outside City Center & Environs of Florence 47
       Arcetri, Campo di Marte area, Carmignano, Fiesole,
       Galluzzo, Impruneta, Montughi, Settignano

VENICE

San Polo & Santa Croce 58

Cannaregio 69

Castello 78

San Marco 92

Dorsoduro 104

Venetian Islands 126
       Giudecca, San Giorgio Maggiore, San Michele,
       Torcello, San Lazzaro degli Armeni

Index of Contributors 132

General Index 138

HOW TO USE THIS BOOK

This is a highly subjective guidebook that reflects the personal tastes and insights of its contributors. We asked architects, painters, writers, and other cultural figures to recommend an overlooked or underappreciated site or artwork, or, alternatively, one that is well-known but about which they could offer fresh insights, personal observations, or specialized information. Respondents were also invited to describe strolls, neighborhoods, events, shops, and all manner of idiosyncratic and traditional ways of spending time in Venice and Florence.

Each map is keyed to the text by numbers. Three icons appear throughout the book to reference restaurants, hotels, and shops.

The editors are delighted with the high number of unusual and inspired recommendations included here. At the same time, we acknowledge that Venice and Florence provide an endless number of rich experiences. It is our hope that you will be inspired by the enthusiasm of our contributors to explore even further and discover secrets of your own.

USEFUL WEBSITES

FLORENCE

Tourism Board of Florence (www.firenzeturismo.it): this official site offers practical information, a calendar of events, information about the city, its museums, parks, villas, etc.

Polo Museale Fiorentino (www.polomuseale.firenze.it): the official website for information about museums and the purchase of tickets to museums.

Florence Net Au (www.florence.net.au): a comprehensive online guide to events, shopping, restaurant, accommodations, etc.

Context Travel (www.contexttravel.com): a network of scholars and specialists who design and lead in-depth walking seminars for small groups of intellectually curious travelers.

VENICE

Tourist Board of Venice (www.turismovenezia.it): information about the city, museums, sites, villas, theater, film, etc.

Comune di Venezia (www.comune.venezia.it): comprehensive guide to events, theater, films, etc.

Fondazione Musei Civici di Venezia (www.museiciviciveneziani.it): information about the city museums (including Doge's Palace and the Museo Correr).

ACTV (www.actv.it): site for public transportation.

Venice Biennale (www.labiennale.org): up-to-date information and events calendar for the contemporary art and architecture exhibitions, and the annual film festival.

Teatro La Fenice (www.teatrolafenice.it): information and tickets to performances at Venice's opera house.

Context Travel (www.contexttravel.com): a network of scholars and specialists who design and lead in-depth walking seminars for small groups of intellectually curious travelers.

FLORENCE & ENVIRONS
HISTORIC CENTER

1 Santa Maria del Fiore
2 Arciconfraternita della
  Misericordia
3 Orsanmichele
🍴 4 Caffè Rivoire
5 Galleria degli Uffizi
6 Società Canottieri
  (Circolo Canottieri)
7 Ponte Vecchio

OLTRARNO

8 Santa Felicita
🎁 9 Madova
🍴 10 Le Volpi e l'Uva
11 Museo Stefano Bardini
12 Boboli Garden
13 Museo La Specola
🍴 14 Piazza Santo Spirito
15 Santa Maria del Carmine

CITY CENTER WEST

🎁 16 N'uovo
17 Refettorio della Chiesa
  di Ognissanti
18 Santa Maria Novella
🍴 19 Trattoria Garga
🍴 20 Il Latini
21 Santa Trinita

CITY CENTER NORTH

🎁 22 Mercato Centrale
🍴 23 Antica Gelateria Fiorentina
24 San Lorenzo
25 Cappelle Medice
26 Palazzo Medici-Riccardi
🏨 27 Hotel Orto de' Medici
28 Opificio delle Pietre Dure
29 Museo Archeologico

CITY CENTER EAST

30 Flood Marker
31 Fondazione Horne
32 Santa Croce
🍴 33 Dolci e Dolcezza

COLLI

34 Piazzale Michelangelo
35 San Miniato al Monte

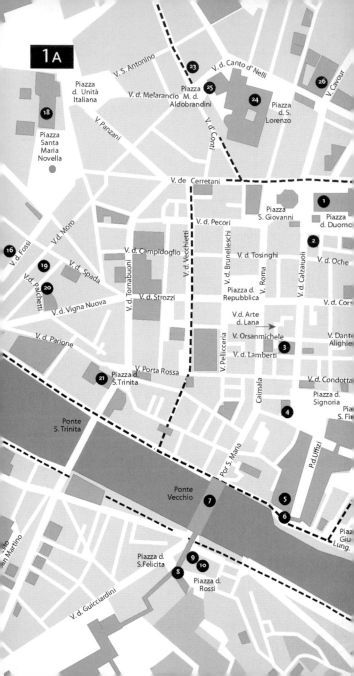

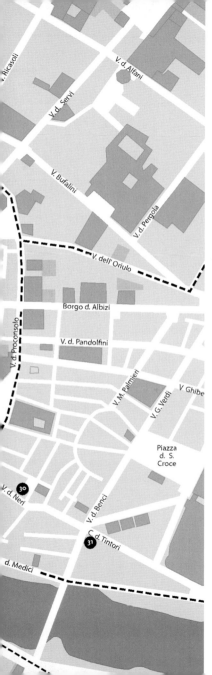

FLORENCE

HISTORIC CENTER

1 Santa Maria del Fiore
2 Arciconfraternità della
  Misericordia
3 Orsanmichele
🍴♀ 4 Caffè Rivoire
5 Galleria degli Uffizi
6 Società Canottieri
7 Ponte Vecchio

OLTRARNO

8 Santa Felicita
🏨 9 Madova
🍴♀ 10 Le Volpi e l'Uva

CITY CENTER WEST

🍴♀ 16 N'uovo
18 Santa Maria Novella
🍴♀ 19 Trattoria Garga
🍴♀ 20 Il Latini
21 Santa Trinita

CITY CENTER NORTH

24 San Lorenzo
25 Cappelle Medicee
26 Palazzo Medici-Riccardi

CITY CENTER EAST

30 Flood Marker
31 Fondazione Horne

FLORENCE

HISTORIC CENTER

1.1 Santa Maria del Fiore (Duomo)
Piazza del Duomo
☎ 055 230 28 85; www.duomofirenze.it
The dome is closed on Sundays.

Dome

1418–1468, Filippo Brunelleschi

How does one begin to describe the achievement that this structure represents? It is no less than the most innovative architectural solution since (and probably including) antiquity. I know of no other building in which form and function are so completely unified.

Brunelleschi inherited certain problems and dimensions from the existing cathedral plan, begun by Arnolfo di Cambio in 1296. His solution was technologically unprecedented, while succeeding, at the same time, in harmonizing an existing Gothic structure with an uncompromisingly modern form. The expanse at the crossing was equivalent to that of the Pantheon, but the Pantheon was a simple poured-concrete dome (a negative form was built in wood, and then cement, mixed sequentially with travertine, brick, and pumice, was poured in). Even though the Pantheon supports no weight at the top—the oculus not only supplies the sole source of light, but also neatly avoids the problem of carrying weight at the most critical point— it developed serious cracks soon after completion.

Brunelleschi instead proposed to build his dome in masonry—the largest ever attempted until that point— and he proposed to do it *without the use of any template forms or scaffolding*. It was to be self-supporting during the construction and surmounted by a massive lantern whose enormous weight is unmatched in any dome before or since, including Michelangelo's for Saint Peter's in Rome. Brunelleschi understood that hemisphere domes tend to fail consistently at around thirty degrees (he had walked to Rome to study the Pantheon) and deduced that sixty degrees, the curvature of Santa Maria del Fiore, was the maximum arc that could support weight from above without deforming.

Brunelleschi's early decision to retain the octagonal perimeter shape left by Arnolfo was critical, and several important features of the construction derive from this choice. The raising of the *tamburo*, or drum section, not only emphasized the importance of the corners, it also made possible the insertion of the huge circular windows in the center of each bay. These windows obviously increase the light to the interior, but more important, the upper curves act as blind arches that transfer the weight of the dome to the corners and down through the piers to the ground. The three smaller domes of the transepts and apse, together with their solid buttresses, help to contain the outward thrust.

Many architects and architectural historians have overlooked the importance of the corners to the dome's engineering. A certain herringbone bricklaying technique, characteristic of circular "rotation" domes, has led to the erroneous conclusion that the dome really functions by virtue of the circle inscribed within the octagon. The herringbone bricklaying technique consists in laying some bricks flat and, periodically, others on edge. Each successive layer is shifted to fit against the previous edge-laid brick, and so on. The adjacent rows of edge-laid bricks result in several vertically spiraling courses through the walls, which converge at the top; the weight of the lantern then tightens the entire structure. An added feature of this technique is that two edge-laid bricks can act as stops, which prevent the other bricks from falling into the void during construction.

The edge-laid rows can occur at intervals roughly equivalent to the arm span of a single worker and can greatly
expedite the construction—especially in this case, where no
scaffolding was used.

The bays between each of the eight ribs of the dome
are flat, and this is a fundamental principle of the building
system Brunelleschi devised here. It is based upon straight-
line transmission of the forces. The weight of the materials
is pulled in toward the void from the corners but it is
opposed by the straight line of force through the flat bays
to the rib on either side. If each bay had been curved outward (to form a circular dome), the opposing forces would
tend to rupture the wall between the ribs. Corners, then,
and flat bays are essential to the support of the dome. This
building is a machine that constantly generates the forces it
needs to support itself.

Aesthetically, the lantern gathers the major formal
lines of the structure, but it also serves an important static
function, as noted above. The average marble block for
it weighs over six thousand pounds. Brunelleschi realized
the importance of the lantern for the stability of the dome.
Although he was present at Signa for the arrival of the first
block shipped from Carrara and accompanied it to Florence
to be hoisted and set in place, he feared he would not live
to see the lantern's completion. Before his death in 1446,
he entrusted the plans to his rival, Michelozzo—who had
beaten him in the competition to build Palazzo Medici—
because he knew he was the only other person capable
of the job.

The cupola occupied Brunelleschi from the earliest
models in 1417 until his death; he supervised every aspect
of its design and construction. He was not merely an
aesthetician (like Alberti, the architect of Santa Maria
Novella a generation later, who couldn't be bothered with
the mechanics of the building process and simply handed
over his drawings to Rossellino to get the work done).
Brunelleschi designed the shape of the bricks (the wooden

forms still exist in the Museo dell'Opera del Duomo) and routinely inspected them for quality as they came out of the ovens in the morning. He designed tools and templates for construction details and even invented several ingenious systems with pulleys for hoisting material up to the building site, since there was no scaffolding from the ground. (Fifty years later, Leonardo da Vinci drew copies of these mechanical devices, and he is often miscredited with their invention.) He made special allowances for drainage and the eventual settling of the ground. The seventy-two holes (three rows of three in each of the eight sections) serve to equilibrate the temperature inside and outside the dome, so that different expansion and contraction rates of the materials would not cause fissures. He even had kitchens installed between the inner and outer domes so that less time would be lost to meal breaks.

Brunelleschi met with considerable resistance along the way. His drawings and plans were notoriously sketchy because he was afraid they would be copied, and twice he nearly lost competitions for this reason. Even though he won the dome competition, Ghiberti was initially named *capomaestro* with him. After numerous disagreements about the construction, Brunelleschi famously feigned sickness and told Ghiberti to go ahead alone. It quickly became apparent that without Brunelleschi, construction would have to cease. Brunelleschi agreed to return only if he was given complete authority over all aspects of the construction. Unbelievably, in 1433, after thirteen years as *capomaestro*, Brunelleschi was arrested for working as a builder without having been matriculated in the mason's guild.

The construction of the dome dominated the civic landscape for fifty years, and it could be seen from as far away as Prato. Even today it inspires awe, especially as one approaches it from the narrow via dello Studio, where it looms above the rooftops, or gazes at it from the lush lawn at the Forte di Belvedere at sunset. Few extant buildings come anywhere near symbolizing civic pride and ambition, or, indeed, human potential and nobility, as much as this great dome.

GEORGE BISACCA
Conservator of paintings

The best four-hundred-and-sixty-three steps to climb in Florence are those ascending Brunelleschi's dome of the cathedral. There is no elevator, but one is amply rewarded for the physical exertion. A small display on one of the landings exhibits Brunelleschi's pulleys and scaffolds used to construct the massive *cupolone*. Upon arriving at a catwalk at the base of the dome, one can view Vasari's painted *Last Judgment* in terrifying proximity. Scaling the spiral staircase toward the summit, notice the herringbone pattern of the brickwork, used to reinforce the dome. The staircase is sandwiched between two interlocking shells, another of Brunelleschi's architectural inventions to make the dome less heavy and self-supporting. The view from Michelozzo's lantern at the top is unequaled in all of Florence. One can see Alberti's Renaissance façade of Santa Maria Novella attached to the Gothic church behind it; the open, square atrium of Palazzo Medici; the Romanesque church of San Miniato perched high on a hill on the other side of the Arno; and the dome of the Synagogue, all with crystalline clarity.

KATEY BROWN
Art historian

Roman Roads

How easy it is to overlook ancient Roman Florence as one strolls through the Renaissance city! Yet the ancient city is very much in evidence in the urban layout: via Torta and via Bentaccordi outline a portion of the Roman amphitheater, and the ancient cardo and decumanus survive as streets that meet at the site of the ancient Roman forum, now the nineteenth-century Piazza della Repubblica. On via Calimala, near the corner of via Por Santa Maria, ask the portiére to see the strada romana; in the basement of this apartment house, not far from Ponte Vecchio, you can see the ruts in the ancient Roman road at the gate that led south out of Florence, toward Rome. This fragment of ancient life was discovered after World War II, when this area was excavated after being mined.

ANN THOMAS WILKINS

Classicist

ITINERARY:

1. Via Torta and Via Bentaccordi, near Santa Croce (City Center East)
2. Piazza della Repubblica (Historic Center)
3. Via Calimala (Historic Center)

1.2 Arciconfraternita della Misericordia
Piazza del Duomo 19/20

I was curious about the Brotherhood of the Misericordia, and it has become my custom to look for them outside their headquarters whenever I visit Florence. Seeing the members emerge from their building in black, hooded robes is certainly a throwback to the brotherhood's founding more than seven hundred and fifty years ago. The hoods help both male and female members remain anonymous as they go about their altruistic work, which includes providing ambulance service in the city.

MARY ANN HAICK DINAPOLI

Historian and genealogist

1.3 Orsanmichele
1361
Via dell'Arte della Lana
☎ 055 238 85; www.polomuseale.firenze.it

Tabernacle
1349–1359, Andrea Orcagna

Though 1337 is the date of Orsanmichele's foundation stone, the building (a granary) was constructed in

1307–1308 and repaired in 1321 and 1332. The critical date, however, is 1361, when the grain market was moved elsewhere and the ground floor transformed into a Marian oratory. (The upper two stories continued in use as granaries. Years ago, a colleague told me that while she was scrambling around up there, examining the structure, she found some kernels of grain.)

Orcagna's tabernacle has been gloriously restored; it includes reliefs of Mary's life, including the death and Assumption of the Virgin. Inside the tabernacle, on the altar, is Bernardo Daddi's *Madonna Enthroned*. The outside of Orsanmichele has some of the greatest works of fifteenth-century Florentine sculpture (though some have now been replaced by replicas, with the originals moved to the Bargello). Among the most notable are Ghiberti's *John the Baptist*; Donatello's *Saint George* and *Saint Mark*, the latter of which Michelangelo praised as representing an honest man—evidently something noteworthy in his experience; Verocchio's *Doubting Thomas* group; and Nanni's *Four Crowned Saints*. The niches themselves are wonderful, especially George's, with its (copy of) Donatello's *schiacciato*, or flattened (the word is also used to describe certain kinds of sandwich) relief of Saint George and the dragon. (The original is in the Bargello.)

RONA GOFFEN
The late Rona Goffen was an art historian.

1.4 Caffè Rivoire

Piazza della Signoria

☎ 055 21 44 12; www.rivoire.it

🍽 Each time we return to Florence we stop at the elegant Caffè Rivoire on Piazza della Signoria for *cioccolata con panna*, piping hot chocolate with heavy whipped cream spread on the top. It's scalding, thinner and less creamy than you might expect, and exceptionally rich in flavor. It's great on a damp winter day and refreshing on a chilly summer evening, but whatever the weather, it's a treat not to be missed; if you stand rather than sit, you can afford to come back for a second.

DAVID G. WILKINS AND ANN THOMAS WILKINS
Art and architectural historian, classicist

Stop at the renowned café on the Piazza della Signoria to enjoy a hot chocolate. It has the most amazing consistency, like the Arno when the water is low.

SUSAN KLEINBERG
Artist

1.5 Galleria degli Uffizi

Piazzale degli Uffizi
☎ 055 238 86 51; www.polomuseale.firenze.it
Closed Mondays. Check the website for hours.
The corridor can accommodate only a limited number of visitors.
Tickets are available online or at the Uffizi ticket office:
☎ 055 29 48 83

Il Corridoio Vasariano
1565, Giorgio Vasari

The corridor of Vasari is a most unusual moment of architecture. Constructed in only five months for a Medici wedding in the year 1565, it was, in effect, devised as a "skyway" or elevated corridor to connect the Palazzo degli Uffizi (formerly the official administrative offices for the Medicis) to the grounds of the Palazzo Pitti on the other side of the Arno.

Elusive and almost disguised—unless one is aware of it—the *corridoio* snakes around and negotiates Florence, transforming itself as it comes into contact with the urban fabric. So where does one find access to this linear architecture? One must go to a stair between Room XXV and Room XXXIV of the Uffizi (make a reservation at the ticket booth). The stair descends through a part of the Uffizi, and suddenly one realizes one is on an enclosed bridge crossing over the Lungarno, with traffic charging along below. This bridge makes a right-angle turn and transforms into the upper, enclosed level of a portico that parallels the Arno! You've probably walked through this portico looking to the Arno, but not realized that above is a passageway for people. And what is more amazing is that the corridor/portico makes yet another sharp turn, to the left this time, to metamorphose into an upper level to the Ponte Vecchio! Once the corridor/bridge traverses the Arno, it "disappears" into a medieval house and emerges to wrap around a medieval tower. And if this isn't enough, the corridor straightens out again and adheres to the front of the Church of Santa Felicita to be incorporated into the church's exterior façade; inside the church, the corridor presents itself as a viewing loggia, so that the Medici princes could see into Santa Felicita. From here the corridor embeds itself between medieval buildings paralleling the via Guicciardini to descend and transform into a staircase that mysteriously becomes a doorway leading out into the Boboli Garden of the Palazzo Pitti. Interestingly enough, one emerges to the sound of water, adjacent to a rather fantastically shell-encrusted grotto. Think about it: the city and garden are joined by a "line" that wiggles and changes its identity (stair, portico, bridge, church façade from without, church viewing box from within, stair again) as it maneuvers the views of a city to become the views and sounds of a garden.

The corridor is lined with not-so-exciting portraits, but this is really not important. What is significant is to make the journey and become part of a portico, part of a bridge (and what a bridge!), part of a church; a line transforming.

JUDITH DIMAIO
Architect

1.6 ## Società Canottieri (Circolo Canottieri)
Early 20th century
Lungarno Maria Luisa de'Medici 8
☎ 055 21 10 93; www.canottierifirenze.it

Built at the beginning of the twentieth century beneath
Giorgio Vasari's sixteenth-century Piazzale degli Uffizi, the
Società Canottieri (known more commonly as the Circolo
Canottieri) is one of the most fascinating spots to experience Florence from a different point of view. This is not the
view of the river from the Ponte Vecchio, or the cityscape
from Piazzale Michelangelo, or the aerial panorama from
the Campanile di Giotto in Piazza del Duomo, but relaxing
in the sun in this flowered garden, one has the privilege of
watching the city as if from its bellybutton. It's no coinci-
dence that among rowing club members the place is
called *l'ombelico*.

The club was established at the beginning of the last
century and holds some prestige in international rowing
circles. It occupies the undercrofts of the Uffizi Palace,
and the beautiful wooden boats run under the Loggia
degli Uffizi and along the river toward the Ponte Vecchio.
Although most of the club is open only to members, no one
will stop you from having a drink at the bar or from taking
a picture of the fascinating boat-gallery or Ponte Vecchio,
where groups of envious tourists might watch you!
FRANCESCA DELL'ACQUA
Art historian

1.7 ## Ponte Vecchio

If you wander across the bridge in the early morning or late
evening when the shops are closed, you can see how the
Florentine symbol of the stylized lily has been adapted as the
decorative pattern for the hinges on the wooden shutters.
DAVID G. WILKINS
Art and architectural historian

OLTRARNO

1.8 Santa Felicita
Piazza Santa Felicita

Annunciation and Deposition
1525–1528, Jacopo Pontormo
Cappella Capponi

On the way to the Palazzo Pitti, immediately after crossing
the Ponte Vecchio, one finds the unassuming church of
Santa Felicita. The church, originally built in the Middle
Ages and remodeled in the middle of the eighteenth century, sits in Firenze's quieter Oltrarno neighborhood, a
neighborhood that is still populated by many of the city's
finest craftsmen and artisans. After entering Santa Felicita,
look into Brunelleschi's marvelous Cappella Capponi
immediately on the right. It is difficult to avoid swooning
when confronted with Jacopo Pontormo's stunning
frescoes. The colors in the *Deposition* are a sumptuous
array of pinks, greens, ochers, and blues. The dead Christ
appears to be in a peaceful slumber as He is passed down
to a crouching figure whose torso magically changes hue
from fuchsia to lime green. Pontormo's wonderful
Annunciation is also located in this chapel. The rapport
between hovering angel and Virgin is sublime!
FRED WESSEL
Artist

In Santa Felicita, in the heart of Florence, art lovers will
find an unlikely oasis of peace and solitude in which to
reflect on two beautiful Pontormos. The tiny chapel, just
inside on the right, houses both the *Annunciation* (fresco)
and the *Deposition* (oil). Here, in one spot, are the first
and last chapters of a great religious tale.

  The works reveal Pontormo's genius with color, going
from hot pink to cool blue, passing from acid green to
warm purple, and creating *chiaroscuro*—a sense of light

and dark—by juxtaposing warm and cool colors without using black.

In an exhibit a year after the 1966 flood of Florence, the *Annunciation* was shown in the Fortezza da Basso. The angel Gabriel and Virgin Mary, on separate sections, were placed side by side as they are in the chapel. As I looked at the two figures I had a disturbing sensation, because I had never noticed before that the two figures are illuminated by different light sources. Gabriel is illuminated from the right and Mary from the left. In their proper settings in the Cappella Capponi, there is a window between them that illuminates the two figures in such a natural manner that one never even considers the light source. Seeing this fresco out of its proper space distorted the artist's intent and prompted me to wonder how often we encounter works of art out of their original contexts.

Happily, in this chapel, we can enjoy these great treasures as the artist intended.

SWIETLAN NICHOLAS KRACZYNA
Artist and printmaker

In spite of the iron fence rail that partially blocks your view, a visit to Pontormo's *Deposition* of Christ in Santa Felicita is a revelation. Christ's heavy body sinks downward as He is lifted and carried. The Virgin swoons.

If you tip the watchman, he may open the cage and let you in to gaze unfettered by the fencing. He likes it best if you pre-book the opportunity—drop by in the morning to enter the chapel later the same day.

DANA PRESCOTT
Artist and writer

In my opinion, Pontormo's *Pietà* (also called *Deposizione*) is possibly the greatest single work in Florence, the *Primavera* of Botticelli notwithstanding. Note, too, the surrounding frescoes.

JOHN C. LEAVEY
Painter

The brilliant and shocking colors, the beautifully strange faces, and the evocative subject matter contribute to this painting's fascination.

LIDIA MATTICCHIO BASTIANICH
Chef, cookbook author, and restaurateur

This church is right across the Ponte Vecchio; on a hot day, after lunch, it's a great spot for a visit, and the painting is fabulous! The vivid colors, the beautiful and harmonious composition. It's a wow. I take everyone who visits us to see it. There's nothing else to see in this church—what a relief!

🍽   Lunch is at Cammillo (Borgo San Jacopo 57R, ☎055 21 24 27), or the trendy Beccofino (Piazza degli Scarlatti 1R, ☎055 29 00 76), where the food is great.

KATHE DYSON
Vintner

1.9 Madova
Via Guicciardini 1/R
☎055 239 65 26; www.madova.com
Closed Sundays.

🎁   After you've visited Santa Felicita for Pontormo's frescoes and *Pietà* altarpiece—and perhaps had a bite to eat at one of the two quite good restaurants to the left and right of the square next to the church—it's an easy stroll to the Palazzo Pitti. On your way there, be sure to stop at Madova, the best glove store in Florence.

RONA GOFFEN
The late Rona Goffen was an art historian.

1.10 Le Volpi e l'Uva
Piazza dei Rossi 1/R
☎055 239 81 32; www.levolpieluva.com

🍽   After drinking in Pontormo's dazzling colors go to the Volpi e l'Uva, a quiet wine bar, and drink in some of Italy's other great art, a glass of its magnificent *vino*. This tranquil oasis is located in the Piazza dei Rossi right next to the church. Sit under an umbrella and order a glass of Tignanello, Barolo, Brunello, or one of the fifteen or so bottles that are opened daily and are available by the glass. Complement this with an order of assorted bread or *focaccia*, an order of assorted salami, and an order of assorted cheeses.

FRED WESSEL
Artist

1.11 Museo Stefano Bardini

Piazza dei Mozzi
☎ 055 234 24 27; www.museicivicifiorentini.it
Open Saturdays, Sundays, and Mondays.

Part of the collection of the early twentieth-century antiquarian Stefano Bardini, in a handsome setting near the Arno, the Museo Bardini is one bridge down from the Ponte Vecchio, half a block in from the bank opposite the Uffizi. The collection includes carvings, sculpture, and decorative art from the medieval period to the Baroque.

HELEN COSTANTINO FIORATTI
Antiques dealer

Shopping Spree

I always check into the Hotel Lungarno. It's a charming, ever-so-discreet, and wonderfully located hotel paralleling the Arno on the Palazzo Pitti side, between the Ponte Vecchio and Ponte Santa Trinita. After checking in, I always follow the same route to a divine sequence of shops. First I go to Castorina, artisans of wood objects since 1895. The shop is on the via Santo Spirito, an extension of the Borgo San Jacopo, so only a slight distance from the Hotel Lungarno. Anyway, it is chock full of architectural details, moldings, simulated marble frames in all shapes and sizes . . . circles, ovals, squares, frames for fans. Gilded reading stands, spheres and obelisks painted to simulate malachite, and a thousand other intriguing objects can be found in this special shop.

Departing this shop, I retrace my steps and cross to Ponte Santa Trinita. When I reach the other side I always turn right and go to Romanelli. For those who love marble and stone, from malachite to lapis lazuli, this store is bliss. There one can find boxes, paperweights, pyramids, urns, spheres, obelisks of the most beautiful craftsmanship, and in the most exquisite marbles, alabasters, and stone. The shop has been around for a very long time, and survived the great flood of 1966.

Once I am able to make the retreat from this shop, which closes for lunch, I retrace my steps to the Ponte Santa Trinita and continue along the Arno to Peter Bazzanti and Son. This is the bronze store where all ancient Roman bronzes from Pompeii, Herculaneum, and just about any other site can be found in reproduction. These bronzes at Bazzanti are of great quality. There are bronze fauns, satyrs, pans, gods, goddesses; busts of Socrates, Homer, and emperors; and bronzes of Antinous and Mithras, to name a few. If you love antiquity and the figural material that populated ancient Roman architecture, you will be in heaven in this wonderful Florentine bottega.

Yet my walk is still not complete. There is one more stop—the large medieval palace at the end of the via Tornabuoni that is closest to the Ponte Santa Trinita. This palazzo is the home of Salvatore Ferragamo, the great shoe designer. Although the store is wonderful, my true interest is in the Museo Salvatore Ferragamo. You must make an appointment at the store to visit the museum, which exhibits all of his great shoe designs and their lasts (blocks or forms in the shape of someone's foot). There, beautifully displayed on the top floor, are shoes that belonged to Audrey Hepburn, Wally Simpson, Judy Garland, Marlene Dietrich, citizens and travelers who found their way to Ferragamo. It is a beautifully appointed museum, and if you love shoes you will not be disappointed.

I always end this walk, or take a luncheon intermezzo before Ferragamo, and it is always to the most lovely Cantinetta Antinori, which is at the opposite end of the via Tornabuoni from the Ponte Santa Trinita. One must pass through a huge arched doorway into a large room much like a cantina. The menu is special every day and it is not a large menu, but once one discovers this delightful Tuscan ambience, it will be hard to go elsewhere.

It is quite amazing when one realizes that in such a small area as I have described, so many varied and intriguing places exist. But this is Florence.

JUDITH DiMAIO

Architect

ITINERARY:

1. Hotel Lungarno Borgo San Jacopo 14, ☎055 272 61
2. Castorina, Via Santo Spirito 13/15R, ☎055 21 28 85
3. Romanelli, Lungarno Acciaiuoli 74/R, ☎055 239 60 47
4. Peter Bazzanti and Son, Lungarno Corsini 46/R
   ☎055 21 56 49
5. Museo Salvatore Ferragamo, Via Tornabuoni 2
   ☎055 336 04 56; www.museoferragamo.it
6. Cantinetta Antinori Piazza Antinori 3, ☎055 292 234;
   www.cantinettaantinori.com. Closed Saturdays and Sundays.

1.12   Boboli Garden (Giardino di Boboli)

Piazza de'Pitti

☎ 055 238 87 86; www.polomuseale.firenze.it

Closed the first and last Monday of every month.

Pack a picnic and spend an afternoon in the Boboli
Garden. Allow at least a few hours.

JOHN L. WONG
Managing principal of SWA Group

Grotta Grande del Buontalenti

1557, begun by Vasari; 1583–1588, completed by Buontalenti

Grotticina di Madama

1553–1555, Davide Fortini and Marco del Tasso

The artificial grotto or *nymphaeum*—a supernatural grotto
space dedicated to the nymphs or muses—was an architectural folly of the Renaissance that took as its reference the
ancient *nymphae* of Rome. Artificial grottoes of the
Renaissance were designed by the leading architects of
the day and incorporated shell encrustations, stalactites,
mosaic, and fantastic sculptural elements. Fountains and
water jokes were integral to the plan, most often placed
in remote parts of the gardens of villas and *palazzi*. Two
of the most well-known, the Grotta Grande and the Grotta
delle Capre in Giardino di Madama, are hidden in the
corners of the Boboli Garden and are well worth seeking
out. Just outside the city, the Villa and Parco Demidoff has
another of the most fabulous grottoes of this kind: the
Apennine fountain and grotto, a giant figure of stalactite
and stone emerging from a small pond, complete with a
shell- and stone-decorated interior.

LESLIE RAINER
Wall-paintings conservator

1.13 Museo La Specola

Via Romana 17
📞 055 228 82 51; www.oapd.inaf.it and www.msn.unifi.it
Tickets must be acquired at the Oratorio San Michele,
Piazzetta San Michele. Closed Mondays.

Tucked into a side road south of the Palazzo Pitti, through
a dark courtyard, and up three flights of stairs: La Specola
—"the Observatory." Florentines know it: they come as
schoolchildren to this surpassingly strange, disconcerting
museum unlike any other. Part is a hodgepodge collection
of taxidermy, gorillas, quetzals, and tapeworms in one
silent room after another. The eerie displays smell faintly
of preservative, and the visitor wanders in solitude. But
this is only the beginning; La Specola's true treasure is
waxworks. Since the collection's beginning in 1775, past
the death of its founder, Grand Duke Pietro Leopoldo di
Lorena, in 1792, and through much of the nineteenth century, the collection has continued to grow. The Grand
Duke founded the museum as a way to teach anatomy
without using corpses. The result is far more violent, a
fantasy of vivisection. Beautifully and artfully made models
of naked, serene people—disemboweled, dissected,
skinned, decomposing—gaze with open and expressive
eyes at the visitor. In one corner are perfect dioramas of
plague-filled streets and syphilis wards. A man's head, eyes
open, goatee, half his skull peeled away. Bring the kids.
SALLIE TISDALE
Writer

Museo La Specola is in the *sezione di zoologia* of the
Museo di Storia Naturale dell'Università di Firenze.
It houses twenty-six full-length wax models and hundreds
of anatomical parts in an eighteenth-century gallery. The
collection is staggering: exquisite, and awe-inspiring.
GERALDINE ERMAN
Artist

1.14   Piazza Santo Spirito

Osteria Santo Spirito
Piazza Santo Spirito 16/R
☎ 055 238 23 83; www.osteriasantospirito.it

Pensione Sorelle Bandini
Piazza Santa Spirito 9; ☎ 055 21 53 08

A walk through Piazza Santo Spirito, especially at dusk, provides one of the most inspiring combinations of space with architecture, as the strange and austere façade of the church fills the space. The Osteria Santo Spirito, on the corner, serves delicious, affordable food in a dark, intimate, shabby-chic atmosphere. Pensione Sorelle Bandini, in a lovely fifteenth-century palazzo, is perfectly placed. The rooms are as big as you can get in Florence, some with a great view over the Arno to the mountains. Cats roam freely through the *pensione*, and a loggia overlooks the piazza.

LESLIE RAINER
Wall-paintings conservator

1.15   Santa Maria del Carmine
Piazza del Carmine 14
Closed Tuesdays.

Cappella Brancacci
15th-century frescoes

A visual experience that cannot be missed is the extraordinary Cappella Brancacci in Santa Maria del Carmine. Literary types will know Masaccio as the "Hulking Tom" at the end of Browning's "Fra Lippo Lippi," a painter who far surpassed the speaker of the poem. Masaccio's frescoes in this chapel were instantaneously legendary for their use of perspective, and if one is to believe the unreliable Vasari, "all the most celebrated sculptors and painters who lived from his day to our own, have become excellent and famous by exercising themselves and studying in this chapel . . . to learn and to grasp the precepts and the rules for good work from the figures of Masaccio." The chapel also contains works by Masolino and, after the deaths of both Masolino and Masaccio, was finished by Filippo Lippi's son, Filippino. In honor of the millennium, a chart now tells you which fresco is which and by whom, but you won't go wrong if you use a method along the lines of Emily Dickinson's litmus test for poetry: if you feel physically as if the top of your head were taken off, you know it's Masaccio. His Adam and Eve expelled from Paradise is as heartbreaking a representation as anything in Western art. And I can never get enough of Saint Peter's curing the sick with his shadow or distributing alms to the poor, though *The Tribute Money* is generally considered the chapel's masterpiece. Masaccio's self-portrait appears underneath it, in a doorway to the right of Saint Peter enthroned. He's the curly-headed one who looks like a wrestler—true to his name, "hulking" or "big bad" Tom.

JACQUELINE OSHEROW
Poet

CITY CENTER WEST

1.16 **N'uovo**
Via dei Fossi 21/R; ☎ 055 504 70 85

Furniture and accessories, gifts, all objects of great imagination and style combining traditional Florentine workmanship with eclecticism and wit. They will make custom pieces and individual items.
HELEN COSTANTINO FIORATTI
Antiques dealer

1.17 **Refettorio della Chiesa di Ognissanti**
Piazza Ognissanti 42
☎ 055 29 48 83; www.polomuseale.firenze.it
Open Mondays, Tuesdays, and Saturdays from 9 a.m. to noon.

The Last Supper
1480, Domenico Ghirlandaio

Although close to many hotels, the Ognissanti is one of the lesser-visited sights in Florence, yet it also contains one of the city's marvels. In the refectory of the monastery is one of Ghirlandaio's most majestic masterpieces, and with any luck you'll have it all to yourself. As was common in refectories, it is a Last Supper that covers the entire end wall. The lush colors, the delicate details (notably the flowers that place the scene in an eternal spring), and the grace of the figures make it a work of art that can enthrall the spectator for many a long, lingering visit. It is one of the most peaceful yet enlivening places in the entire city—an immediate refreshment for even the weariest tourist.
THEODORE K. RABB
Historian

1.18 Santa Maria Novella

Piazza di Santa Maria Novella
📞 055 28 21 87
Closed Fridays.

Trinity
c. 1426, Masaccio
North Aisle

Last Judgment
1354–1357, Nardo di Cione
Cappella Strozzi

Visit Santa Maria Novella for Masaccio's *Trinity* and
Nardo di Cione's *Last Judgment* frescoes. The Strozzi altar-
piece by Nardo's older brother Orcagna is still in situ in
the chapel.
RONA GOFFEN
The late Rona Goffen was an art historian.

1.19 Trattoria Garga

Via del Moro 48; 📞 055 239 88 98

🍴 Fun, great food.
RICHARD L. FEIGEN
Art dealer and collector

1.20 Il Latini

Via dei Palchetti 6/R
📞 055 21 09 16; www.illatini.com

🍴 Slather olive oil on the *ribollita* and devour a steak at a
communal table at Il Latini. No menus, just grouchy wait-
ers and well-dressed Florentines. Rough, but . . .
ROSS ANDERSON
Architect

Cenacoli

I recommend searching out the Cenacoli (Last Suppers) of
Florence, the frescoes that adorn the refectories of
Renaissance monasteries and nunneries. Some are easily
accessible, like the two magnificent and well-preserved
Ghirlandaio Last Suppers in San Marco and Ognissanti.
Some are worth seeking out, such as that by Andrea del
Castagno in the still cloistered nunnery of Sant'Apollonia.
And then there are the lesser-known examples by Perugino
in the Convent of Sant'Onofrio, and the marvelous Andrea
del Sarto in the church of San Salvi. And if you are lucky,
or very persuasive, you might talk the nuns of the Calza
near Porta Romana into letting you briefly glimpse their
precious Cenacolo painted by Franciabigio.

WILLIAM E. WALLACE
Art historian

ITINERARY:

1. Museo di San Marco, Piazza San Marco 1
   ☎055 238 86 08; www.firenzemusei.it
2. Ognissanti Piazza Ognissanti 42
3. Sant'Apollonia, Via XXVII Aprile 1
   ☎055 238 86 07. Closed the second and fourth Monday of
   every month.
4. Sant'Onofrio, Via Faenza 42
5. San Michele a San Salvi, Via di San Salvi 16
6. Il Convento della Calza, Piazza della Calza 6

1.21   ### Santa Trinita
Piazza di Santa Trinita
☎055 21 69 12; www.firenzeturismo.it

Frescoes and Altarpiece
c. 1422, Lorenzo Monaco

Cappella Sassetti
1479–1485, Domenico Ghirlandaio

Visit Santa Trinita for the frescoes and altarpiece, which are the late work of Lorenzo Monaco—and for the Sassetti chapel by Ghirlandaio, likewise with frescoes and altarpiece in situ.

RONA GOFFEN

The late Rona Goffen was an art historian.

CITY CENTER NORTH

1.22 **Mercato Centrale**
Via dell'Ariento 10–14
Open from 7 a.m. to 2 p.m. Closed Sundays.
In winter, only open on Saturdays.

Walk through San Lorenzo market early in the morning,
visiting the fishmongers, butchers, and fruit and vegetable
vendors. There is such energy and enthusiasm here. Then
head over to the church of San Lorenzo and relax in
Brunelleschi's masterpiece.
LIDIA MATTICCHIO BASTIANICH
Chef, cookbook author, and restaurateur

1.23 **Antica Gelateria Fiorentina**
Via Faenza 2a; ☎ 388 058 03 99
Closed Sundays.

As you leave the Mercato Centrale di San Lorenzo—a
fascinating place and worth seeing (only in the mornings)—
you'll find a tiny ice cream shop on the via Faenza, just off
via Sant'Antonio. It is called Antica (though remodeled)
Gelateria Fiorentina. Stop there and try their Nutella ice
cream. (Nutella is the commercial name of the beloved
Italian hazelnut paste. During a Nutella strike several years
ago, the newspapers wrote of desperate mothers who did
not know how to deal with merenda, or snack time. I know
depressed ladies who lie in bed and eat it with a spoon.)
Fiorentina's flavors, when compared to the most famous
ice cream shops in Florence, are a revelation! Also less
expensive and with much bigger scoops, but that's not
the point.
HELEN COSTANTINO FIORATTI
Antiques dealer

1.24 ## San Lorenzo
Piazza di San Lorenzo
www.sacred-destinations.com

Biblioteca Mediceo-Laurenziana
Begun in 1524, Michelangelo
Enter from Cloister.

In the sprawling monastic complex of San Lorenzo, visitors sometimes have difficulty locating Michelangelo's Laurentian Library. From a convoluted approach through an unexceptional cloister and up a dark and narrow stair, the unwary visitor steps into an expansive and impressive volume of vertical space—the Laurentian Library vestibule. As with the nearby Medici Chapel, a dense exterior architecture has been brought indoors. Rising from the shoulders of peculiarly anthropomorphic consoles, paired monolithic columns soar to meet sections of broken entablature. A casual visitor is rendered small in such stately company. The oft-described sense of enclosure and compression in the vestibule is felt mainly when, like a servant, one stands to the side of the monumental staircase or climbs its side wings. To mount the central flight—reserved, said Michelangelo *per il signore*—is to feel like a prince and to experience the grandeur of the Medici, whose purposes Michelangelo well served. From the center of the broad staircase, the vestibule is capacious, the prince its center, the columns his ordered retainers. The consoles genuflect. The vestibule organizes human experience and helps shape the person within it. It is an architecture for princes.
WILLIAM E. WALLACE
Art historian

The overblown scale of the stair in the vestibule, the wall reversal, and the gigantic scale of the columns and volutes make this one of the most compact and rich spaces of the Renaissance.
ROBERT LIVESEY
Architect

One of the most extraordinary moments in architecture, Michelangelo's corner of the stair hall leading to the Laurentian Library is packed with more architectonic power than most entire buildings. A corner that puts Mies van der Rohe to shame, here "more is more" with an almost inexpressible series of spatial operations. Just to name a few: folded space, mirrored space, inside-outside space, layered space, negative space, positive space, warped space. For an architect, the details are literally breathtaking; the mind can barely grasp the way this corner was conceived, let alone built for all to see—and to feel.

ALEXANDER GORLIN
Architect

1.25 ## Cappelle Medicee
Piazza di Madonna degli Aldobrandini
☎ 055 29 48 83; www.polomuseale.firenze.it
Closed on the second and fourth Sunday and first third and fifth Monday of every month.

New Sacristy (Sagrestia Nuova)
1521–1524, Michelangelo

The rough exterior of irregular brick courses of the New Sacristy of San Lorenzo in Florence looks like it was stripped of its façade, but in fact it was never finished. Michelangelo's design remains one of the great unbuilt projects of the world, a complex, interlocking, sculptural façade of columns, pilasters, moldings, and panels. Stand before the façade with a photograph of the original wooden model and imagine the lost grandeur of the absent masterpiece.

ALEXANDER GORLIN
Architect

A space that soars and enlightens the viewer. Try to go there early, when it is quiet.

JOHN L. WONG
Managing principal of SWA Group

Sotterraneo

1529–1530, Michelangelo

☎ 055 238 86 02

By appointment at the ticket office.

Each year I bring groups of artists to Italy to paint and study the Italian Renaissance. One of the visits that moves the romantics among us to tears is the little-known *sotterraneo* under the Sagrestia Nuova at San Lorenzo. Here are recently discovered wall drawings in the secret passageway where Michelangelo hid from the Medici for three days during the 1530 siege of Florence. Having sided with the Republic against the exiled Medici (another chapter in the love-hate relationship between Michelangelo and the most famous art patrons of all time), he feared the consequences of his perceived betrayal. While in hiding he took some pitch from a wall torch and, as he later wrote, "to forget my fears I fill these walls with drawings."

Standing among the drawings, sketches, and doodles (yes, even doodles!) that cover the walls and ceilings of this tiny cave-like structure, one feels as if one is on tour inside Michelangelo's mind. It is "virtual Michelangelo."

To enter, you must ask for an additional ticket to the *sotterraneo* when purchasing the standard ticket to the Medici Tombs. The ticket you receive will be a timed admission to the passageway. Upon entering the Sagrestia Nuova you will notice, at the far side of the room, a small, plain-looking door with a guard standing next to it. At the designated time present him with the second ticket and enter this most magical of places.

Fred Wessel
Artist

The drawings were made by Michelangelo and a few others during the Spanish invasion of 1529–1530. It's wonderful to scan the walls, seeing what you can and imagining the rest, while footsteps echo overhead.

Susan Kleinberg
Artist

1.26   Palazzo Medici-Riccardi

15th century, Michelozzo; major addition at the end of the
17th century
Via Cavour, ☎ 055 276 03 40

Procession of the Magi

1459–1463, Benozzo Gozzoli
Admission to the chapel in small groups.

Years ago, before the restoration, when there was no ticket
booth, no gift shop, and no locked wrought-iron gate in
the entryway, I used to find it impossible to be on the via
Cavour, or, indeed, anywhere near the Palazzo Medici-
Riccardi, without running into the courtyard and up the
steps to spend at least a few minutes taking in Benozzo
Gozzoli's *Procession of the Magi*. There I'd be at the bus
stop, late for someone or something, but I'd decide that I
couldn't live until I remembered how many cheetahs
appeared in the procession (two—but one looks a little like
a bobcat), or refreshed my mind as to the precise nature of
the golden discs hanging from the ornamental regalia on
Cosimo de'Medici's horse.

Everyone responds to these frescoes. I've brought
nineteen-month-olds ("See the horsey? See the monkey?")
and I've brought sober senior-citizen attorneys who couldn't
contain themselves. There are certainly greater works
of art to be seen in Florence, but I know of none more
delightful. (The only one that might give it any competition
at all is Luca Della Robbia's choir loft in the Museo
dell'Opera del Duomo, and by all means don't miss that
either.) There's an undeniable charm in such elaborate and
loving detail; besides, it's always a thrill to see a landscape
at the edges of a fresco that looks precisely like the place
where you took a walk that very morning. (For a view of
countryside just like Gozzoli's, follow signs to the Museo
delle Porcellane in the Boboli Garden, see p. 26; there's a
lovely view from the grounds right beside it.) And even a

rather entrenched non-Christian like myself can get into the spirit of this over-the-top procession. Who doesn't love to bring gifts to newborn babies, even when they're nothing more than human? By the way, Gozzoli himself appears twice in these frescoes. On the east wall, he wears a red hat inscribed with gold block letters, the closest thing the chapel has to a signature: OPUS BENOTTI (a Latin pun on his name, suggesting that his work is "well-noted" or, perhaps, that the viewer should "note it well." I'm indebted to Diane Cole Ahl, who notices this pun in her book *Benozzo Gozzoli*.) On the west wall, he wears a blue hat, with a white band, his fingers displayed in an odd configuration reminiscent of a salutation out of *Star Trek*.

JACQUELINE OSHEROW
Poet

I always stop by the Medici palace to see the *Procession of the Magi* in the little chapel. It's one of my son's favorite stops in all the world, a kind of "Where's Waldo" fresco, abundant with exotic animals and birds.

DANA PRESCOTT
Artist and writer

1.27 Hotel Orto de' Medici

Via San Gallo 30
☏ 055 48 34 27; www.ortodeimedici.it

Though I have stayed in all levels of accommodations in Florence, from student *pensioni* to elegant five-star hotels, my favorite is the lovely Hotel Orto de' Medici (previously the Hotel Splendor), on via San Gallo. The breakfast room of this patrician palace makes me never want to leave, and I have often painted and sketched on the adjoining terrace, which looks out on the Piazza San Marco.

DANA PRESCOTT
Artist and writer

1.28 Opificio delle Pietre Dure

Via degli Alfani 78

☎ 055 28 94 14; www.opificiodellepietredure.it

Florentine mosaics, the *pietre dure* whose traditional combination of marble and precious stones goes back to antiquity, nearly died out during the Middle Ages, at which time the craft was revived by Lorenzo the Magnificent. By the end of the nineteenth century, the popularity of the *pietre dure* had begun to fade again, until the late 1930s when it died out almost completely.

In 1947, Richard Allmand Blow (1904–1985) set up a workshop on his property to revive the art form. (Blow was an American painter who spent several months a year at Villa Piazza Calda, a Renaissance structure he'd bought and restored in 1927; it stood on a hilltop in Santa Margherita a Montici, across the Arno from Florence.) Because of general shortages of materials Blow came to use, and ultimately favor, the gray and ocher stone dug from the riverbed of the Arno, and it became a trademark of some of the more beautiful pictures, boxes, obelisks, and tabletops that survive. Standing on any bridge across the Arno, especially on a wintry day, one can see the same color and opacity of the stone in the water itself.

To see the stone and the mosaics, visit the Opificio delle Pietre Dure on the via degli Alfani, which had been the Monastery of San Nicolò until 1853; it now contains many worthwhile examples, as well as the evidence that *pietre dure* is again a thriving industry in Florence. Richard Blow was a link in this chain.

ADELE CHATFIELD-TAYLOR
President of the American Academy in Rome

1.29 **Museo Archeologico**
Via della Colonna 38
☎ 055 29 48 83; www.firenzemusei.it

Once a dusty, rather unorganized repository of objects
Greek, Roman, Etruscan, and Egyptian, Florence's
Archaeology Museum has been refurbished so that its treasures can be viewed in their cultural contexts. The Greek
red- and black-figured vases—the best-known being the
intricate François krater—and the Etruscan funerary monuments are among my favorites. I am especially drawn to
the solemn, enthroned mother-and-child cinerary urn from
Chianciano (limestone, c. 400 B.C.E.). We don't know
when it was discovered, but it or a similar urn surely
influenced some artists when they depicted the theme of the
Madonna and Child.
ANN THOMAS WILKINS
Classicist

Perhaps the only great museum in Florence where the har-
ried tourist can enjoy peace, quiet, and unobstructed views
of the art is the National Archaeological Museum. Very
much off the beaten tourist track in this Renaissance-
centered city, the museum is nonetheless home to major
monuments that every undergraduate has seen in art history
textbooks. There's the dramatic, snarling Chimera of
Arezzo; the portrait statue of that worthy, weather-beaten
Roman citizen Aulus Metellus, a.k.a. L'Arringatore; the
François vase with its visual encyclopedia of Greek legend
in Attic black-figure painting; and the Etruscan cinerary
urn of a young man accompanied by a kindly but imposing
death-demon. In addition to the well-known works, there
are also dozens of hidden treasures in the cases of bronze
statuettes and pottery that anyone with an interest in antiquity will be delighted to discover.
SUSAN E. WOOD
Art historian

CITY CENTER EAST

1.30 **Flood Marker**
Northwest corner of Via dei Neri and Via San Remigio

The Arno flood of November 4, 1966, was only the most recent in a series of six inundations that date back to 1177. For an original *trecento* marker of the flood of November 1, 1333, go to this corner and look up. A fourteenth-century hand reaches up through the waves, an outstretched finger just touching the high-water mark. For another set of flood markers, see those on the façade of Brunelleschi's Pazzi Chapel, in the cloister at Santa Croce.
DAVID G. WILKINS AND ANN THOMAS WILKINS
Art and architectural historian, and classicist

1.31 **Fondazione Horne**
Via dei Benci 6
℡ 055 24 46 61; www.museohorne.it
Closed Sundays.

Between the Arno and Santa Croce is the personal collection of an expatriate in his former house that boasts among its treasures a superb *Saint Stephen*, tentatively attributed to Giotto.
HELEN COSTANTINO FIORATTI
Antiques dealer

1.32 **Santa Croce**
Piazza di Santa Croce
℡ 055 244 619; www.sacred-destinations.com

Santa Croce is the great Franciscan church of Florence, and one goes there for just everything—Michelangelo's tomb, the Bruni monument (he was buried with a copy of his

History of Florence), and Giotto's Bardi and Peruzzi chapels, inter alia.
RONA GOFFEN
The late Rona Goffen was an art historian.

Frescoes, Bardi Chapel

1371, Giotto

I'd hate for anyone to miss Giotto's depiction of the confirmation of the stigmata in the Bardi Chapel in Santa Croce. Of course, visitors already have innumerable reasons to visit this blockbuster church: the tombs of Michelangelo and Galileo, among other luminaries; Brunelleschi's gem of a Pazzi Chapel and his beautifully proportioned courtyard; not to mention what one of my landladies once referred to as that *poverino*: Cimabue's crucifix, irreparably damaged in the 1966 flood. I'd certainly encourage everyone to see them all—I've spent entire afternoons daydreaming in the Pazzi Chapel—but, for me, what's most affecting in the entire Santa Croce complex are the looks on the faces of Giotto's monks as they hover in attendance on their wounded saint.
JACQUELINE OSHEROW
Poet

Second Cloister

Completed in 1453, after a design by Brunelleschi

I had always admired Brunelleschi's famous dome and Pazzi Chapel in Florence, but emotionally they had never done much for me, seeming mostly like feats of engineering. In Santa Croce's second cloister, I saw how this extraordinary Renaissance architect adapted his style to the Franciscan vision of life, and I began to love his work. Often missed by tourists, it is just a few steps from the Pazzi Chapel.

For me, this cloister is the perfect architectural expression of Franciscan poverty, that lack of things that generates plenitude. The second (higher) register of slender columns frames the air, creates pure squares of space, and etherealizes the square cloister below, whose form they echo. These squares and the solid Romanesque arches with their peaceful rhythm below (in the first register) teach us somehow about Franciscan simplicity, the solidity of simplicity.

After this, one's compelled to reconsider other Brunelleschi structures. The Pazzi Chapel seems a hymn to mind, and the Romanesque arches of the Spedale degli Innocenti, one of Brunelleschi's earlier works, strike us with their rhythm, which seems both beautiful and healing. The dome, of course, is Florence's signature and an expression of her lucky, happy hubris.

JANE OLIENSIS
Cultural historian

1.33 Dolci e Dolcezza
Piazza Cesare Beccaria 8/R
℡ 055 234 66 98

Pastries, gifts and delicious desserts; refined and a real cut above the others. Run by a young man who found himself by founding an unusual place for Italy.

HELEN COSTANTINO FIORATTI
Antiques dealer

The Work of Benedetto da Maiano

Walking through the Palazzo Vecchio, I looked up and saw a beautiful doorway by Benedetto da Maiano. I searched for more of his work and found the pulpit in Santa Croce and a marble bust of Mellini at the Bargello.

BETH VAN HOESEN ADAMS
The late Beth van Hoesen Adams was an artist and a printmaker.

ITINERARY:
1. Palazzo Vecchio, Piazza della Signioria, Sala d'Udienza
2. Santa Croce, Piazza di Santa Croce
3. Bargello Via del Proconsolo 4; www.firenzemusei.it

COLLI

1.34   A Stroll to the Piazzale Michelangelo

Bus to Piazzale Galileo, walk the Viale Galileo, stop at San Miniato al Monte, and on to Piazzale Michelangelo

Everyone knows about the drop-dead gorgeous view of the city from the Piazzale Michelangelo, but getting there can be half the fun if you take a bus up to the Piazzale Galileo and walk from there. Stroll at a leisurely pace up the curving viale Galileo, enjoying many brief glimpses of the city. In spring, the gardens along this route are filled with Florence's trademark irises. Near your destination, pause for a visit to San Miniato al Monte, one of the finest surviving examples of Romanesque architecture in the Tuscan black-and-white style, which for my money is the most beautiful of the Romanesque regional styles in Europe. The church also boasts a stunning apse-mosaic and marble intarsia floors. When you reach the Piazzale Michelangelo, give your feet a well-earned rest and enjoy the view from a café or *gelateria*. Guilty pleasures include the kitschy but colorful souvenir stands.

SUSAN E. WOOD
Art historian

1.35   San Miniato al Monte

Via Monte alle Croci 34
☎ 055 234 27 31; www.sacred-destinations.com

The combination of view and architecture make this an ideal spot to begin or end a visit to Florence. High on a hill overlooking the city, the view encompasses the Arno River, flowing westward toward Pisa, as well as the outlines of the city's major monuments. The green and white marble Tuscan Romanesque façade of the church and the Renaissance Chapel of the Cardinal of Portugal inside reveal the continuing impact of classicism in Florentine

architecture. Try to visit in the late afternoon, when the
sun is setting.
DAVID G. WILKINS
Art and architectural historian

Chapel of the Cardinal of Portugal

Luca della Robbia, Antonio Rossellino, Alesso Baldovinetti,
Antonio and Piero del Pollaiolo

It's hard to imagine a more serene burial chapel than this
one, erected in the 1460s to honor a young cardinal, a
prince from the royal house of Portugal, who died in
Florence in 1459. The chapel is perhaps the most harmonious decorative ensemble of the fifteenth century, with
contributions by della Robbia, Rossellino, Baldovinetti,
Pollaiolo, and others. Notice how the design of the ceiling
matches that of the floor, how the walls are coordinated,
and how the wrought-iron gate is repeated in the painted
altarpiece. Best of all, the landscapes in the paintings
echo the same views we see today as we stand outside the
church and look out over the meandering river and cypress
trees of the local landscape.
DAVID G. WILKINS
Art and architectural historian

OUTSIDE CITY CENTER & ENVIRONS OF FLORENCE

Medici Villas

A good day outing is to see the nearby recommended villas—all within the environs of Florence. Don't forget to pack a picnic.
JOHN L. WONG
Managing principal of SWA Group

One of the wonders of Florence is how accessible the countryside is. I always make at least one foray to see one of the nearby gardens. These are great locations to sketch or paint undisturbed. Easily reached by bus, too.
DANA PRESCOTT
Artist and writer

1. Villa Medicea della Petraia
1576–1589, Buontalenti
Castello, 4 miles north of Florence
www.polomuseale.firenze.it
Closed the second and third Monday of every month.

2. Villa Le Balze
Fiesole, 4 miles northeast of Florence
☏055 592 08; www.villalebalze.org
The gardens are open to the public.

3. Villa Medici (see p. 50)
1458, Michelozzo
Fiesole, 4 miles northeast of Florence
☏055 239 89 94; www.fiesole.com

4. Villa Gamberaia (see p. 54)
1610, Zanobi Lapi and others
Settignano, 5 miles northeast of Florence
☏055 69 72 05; www.villagamberaia.com

5. Villa Medicea

1596, Buontalenti
Artimino, 12 miles west of Florence
☏055 875 14 26; www.artimino.com

6. Villa Medicea

1479, Giuliano da Sangallo
Poggio a Caiano, 14 miles northwest of Florence
☏055 87 70 12; www.polomuseale.firenze.it
Closed Tuesdays, and the second and third Monday of
every month.

The Stones of Italy

The cities of Italy are extrusions of the local geology.
Fashioned from materials readily at hand, every town has
a distinctive character and color: the pervasive salmon of
Assisi; the burnt red of Siena; the terra-cotta of Bologna;
the motley, molding assemblage that is Venice. Florence is
brown, opaque, and unyielding. The streets are canyons of
local *pietra forte*, an unforgiving, roughhewn stone. In this
monochromatic and fundamentally medieval environment,
the new outdoor sculpture of the Renaissance—heroic classical figures in marble and gilt bronze by Ghiberti and
Donatello—must have been dazzling, colorful, modern.

Tucked into the Vincigliata hills near Bernard Berenson's Villa I Tatti is the Luogo delle Colonne, the Renaissance stone quarry where Giorgio Vasari obtained the
monolithic columns that adorn the Uffizi. The abandoned
quarry became a favorite watering hole of Victorians who
dammed the stream, laid out paths, and constructed a
pseudo-Gothic tower in the midst of the glen. Queen
Victoria favored this idyllic retreat, a cool respite from the
Florentine summer. Now, one trespasses private property
to find the crystal pool defiled by trash and stagnation.
WILLIAM E. WALLACE
Art historian

ARCETRI

1 mile south of Florence (not on map)

Trattoria Omero
Via Pian dei Giullari 11/R
☎ 055 22 00 53; www.ristoranteomero.it

🍴 Real Tuscan food, no frills.
RICHARD L. FEIGEN
Art dealer and collector

CAMPO DI MARTE AREA

2 miles northeast of Historic Center (not on map)

Pasticceria Buscioni
Via Cento Stelle 1/R, ☎ 055 60 27 65
Closed Mondays.

🍴 En route to the main road to Fiesole, Buscioni, on the via
Cento Stelle, has the most marvelous warm raised doughnuts.
They are light as a feather and filled either with apricot
preserves or pastry cream; they're available in the morning,
summer and winter, and after 4:30 p.m. in the winter.
They're so good that my steering wheel has had to be treat-
ed with Handi Wipes before I've driven even a few yards.
HELEN COSTANTINO FIORATTI
Antiques dealer

CARMIGNANO

15 miles west of Florence (not on map)

Chiesa di San Michele
Visitation
1530, Jacopo Pontormo

After you've seen Pontormo's *Annunciation* in Santa
Felicita, take an afternoon and drive out to Carmignano
where in San Michele you can see his splendid *Visitation*.
🍴 After that, have a great meal at Da Delfina (via della

Chiesa 1, ☎055 87 18 074; www.dadelfina.it) in Artimino (looking directly at a Medici villa). This is the best Tuscan cooking I know. Carlo Cioni, the owner, is really wonderful. (Delfina is his mother's name.) Sunday lunch is a great time to do this.

KATHE DYSON
Vintner

FIESOLE
4 miles northeast of Florence (not on map)

Villa Medici
1458, Michelozzo
☎055 239 89 94; www.fiesole.com

A Renaissance villa of the Medici sited on the hillside overlooking the city of Florence. A magnificent example of a fifteenth-century villa where the landscape and architecture are as one. A series of terraces steps down the side of the hill connected by gardens, pathways, and stairs. Various views of the city of Florence and surrounding countryside are unveiled along this informal walk. The entrance is inconspicuous; it is a side door on the street side of a walled garden.

JOHN L. WONG
Managing principal of SWA Group

Museo Bandini
Via Giovanni Duprè 1
☎055 596 12 93; www.museidifiesole.it

This two-room museum can be seen while visiting Fiesole and the *teatro Romano*, as it is open during the day without interruption. It shows small, gold-background, jewel-like, primarily Tuscan paintings of the fourteenth and fifteenth centuries, and also a handsome nuptial chest, called a *cassone*.

HELEN COSTANTINO FIORATTI
Antiques dealer

GALLUZZO

3 miles southwest of Florence (not on map)

La Certosa del Galluzzo

1342, Niccolò Acciaioli

Colle di Montaguto

☎ 055 204 92 26; www.abbeys-of-tuscany.com

Outside the village of Galluzzo; a twenty-minute ride on bus no. 37 from Piazza Santa Maria Novella. Best to call ahead.

Frescoes

1522–1525, Jacopo Pontormo

Palazzo degli Studi

For more Pontormo *capolavori* and for a tourist-free art experience, escape to La Certosa Monastery. It is set in a peaceful landscape where even on the hottest day in August you will find a fresh breeze.

La Certosa was built by Niccolò Acciaioli in 1342, and occupied by the Carthusian monks until 1958. Now it is occupied by a dozen or so monks of the Cistercian order, a subgroup of the Benedictines. It can be visited for free, although a good tip will make the trip worth your while. A monk will be your guide.

In the picture gallery of the Palazzo degli Studi are five Pontormo frescoes, painted in the sixteenth century, after he fled to La Certosa to escape a plague in Florence.

Pontormo's five lunettes depict the stages of Christ's Passion. The cycle was originally in the outside courtyard and the paintings have badly weathered; much detail has disappeared. What the frescoes do reveal is the artist's incredible concept of abstract design. To eyes accustomed to twentieth-century art, Pontormo's abstract shapes and his unusual combinations of color are a pure delight.

If you finish your visit at La Certosa and find yourself in search of lunch or dinner, I suggest that you walk back to Via Senese. A further four hundred meters south (toward Siena) will bring you to a group of houses—the

🍴 hamlet of Bottai. The trattoria, La Bianchina (via Cassia 36, ☎ 055 202 21 63; www.labianchina.com), is well-known for its *bistecca Fiorentina* and *pappardelle al cinghiale* (noodles with a heavy wild boar sauce). After the meal, cross the street and take the bus back to Florence.

If your Certosa excursion is by car, you can drive back to Galluzzo for dinner. Head toward Florence, and at the first traffic light, turn left onto via Volterrana. Wind your way up for about two kilometers and on the right side, just

🍴 before the Pieve Giogoli, is a trattoria called Bella Ciao (via Volterrana, ☎ 055 74 15 02). There is no sign, and actually, it is not classified as a trattoria but as a *circolo recreativo* named after two local partisans. Bella Ciao has good wood-baked pizzas, excellent meats, and greaseless, deep-fried vegetables. But their specialty is tripe. If you are into tripe, this is the best place in all of Florence. You can eat tripe as antipasto, *primo*, main course, and I think also as dessert, while you sit outside on a large terrace over-looking the Florentine hills. Keep in mind: they are open only in the evenings, are closed Mondays and Tuesdays, and do not take credit cards.

SWIETLAN NICHOLAS KRACZYNA
Artist and printmaker

IMPRUNETA
8 miles south of Florence (not on map)

Bar Italia
Piazza Buondelmonti 33, ☎ 055 201 10 46

🍴 The ice creams are intensely flavored; I recommend the very dark chocolate and delicious nut flavors and all the fruits, or the hot chocolate in winter. If you get sticky or need to use the bathroom, it's an unexpected dream of marble and luxury.

Impruneta has been famous for terra-cotta for centuries. Try to see the Luca della Robbias in Santa Maria all'Impruneta on Piazza Buondelmonti.

HELEN COSTANTINO FIORATTI
Antiques dealer

MONTUGHI

1 mile north of historic center (not on map)

Museo Stibbert

Via Frederick Stibbert 26, off the via Vittorio Emmanuele
℡ 055 47 55 20; www.museostibbert.it
Closed Thursdays.

Set in an outlying area surrounded by parks, this villa is a good place to take children. You'll immediately recognize the taste of a collector of one hundred years ago—a true time warp—with the late owner's love of arms and armor and full-scale horse models, with their trappings.

HELEN COSTANTINO FIORATTI
Antiques dealer

SETTIGNANO

6 miles northeast of Florence (not on map)

One fascinating spot for enjoying Florentine atmosphere is the hill where the village of Settignano lies. Take the no. 10 bus from the Piazza San Marco; the bus winds up narrow roads and past Tuscan gardens, depositing you finally in a silent and enchanted little square with a small church, a news-agent, and a single bar. Walk around and admire Florence from above.

Settignano is the birthplace of many marble sculptors, the most famous certainly Desiderio. His extraordinarily delicate works can still be seen in Santa Croce, Santa Maria Novella, and other Florentine sites.

For an unconventional descent, try the stone-paved stairs of the pedestrian via Vecchia di Settignano. At the bottom is

Ponte a Mensola, and if you can walk another ten minutes, follow the via di Vincigliata to the fabulous Villa I Tatti. Here the art historian Bernard Berenson spent his life studying Renaissance art and gathering around him not only magnificent artworks of the past, but also the most brilliant intellectuals of his own day.

FRANCESCA DELL'ACQUA
Art historian

Villa Gamberaia

1610, Zanobi Lapi and others
Via Rossellino 72
☎ 055 69 72 05; www.villagamberaia.com

The Villa Gamberaia is well worth the visit, if only to stroll along the cypress-lined Philosopher's Walk and enjoy the framed view of the Florentine landscape beyond. The *giardino segretto* and axial relationships of the garden and villa deserve particular scrutiny.

D. B. MIDDLETON
Architect

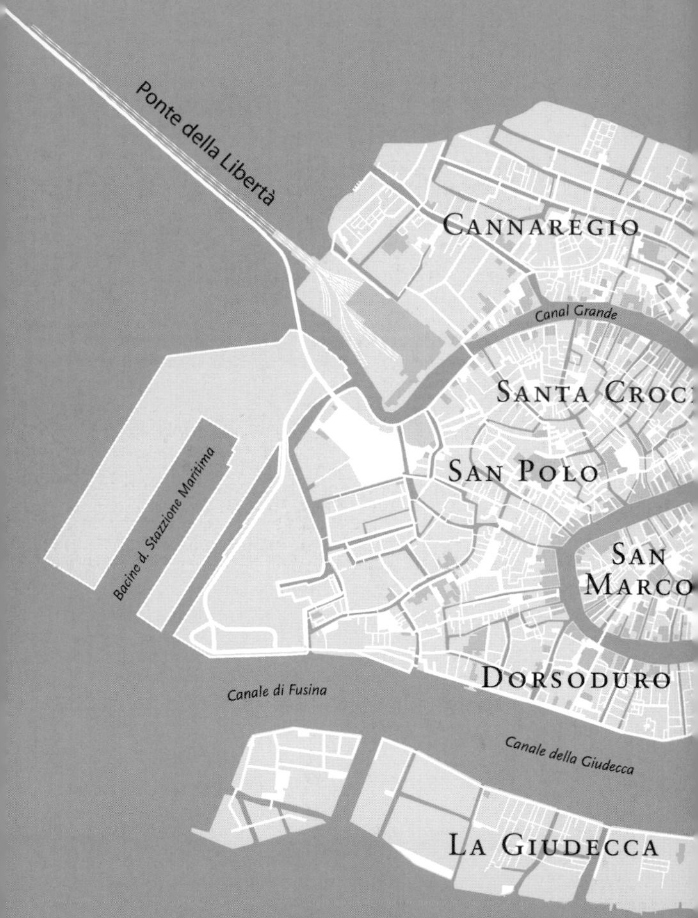

Ponte della Libertà

CANNAREGIO

Canal Grande

SANTA CROCE

SAN POLO

SAN
MARCO

Bacino d. Stazzione Marittima

Canale di Fusina

DORSODURO

Canale della Giudecca

LA GIUDECCA

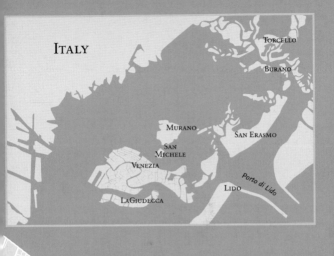

ITALY

TORCELLO

BURANO

MURANO

SAN ERASMO

SAN
MICHELE

VENEZIA

Porto di Lido

LIDO

LAGIUDECCA

CASTELLO

Canale Di San Marco

SAN
GIORGIO
MAGGIORE

VENICE

SAN POLO & SANTA CROCE

1.1 **Istituto Universitaria di Architettura di Venezia**
Campo dei Tolentini
www.iuav.it

Entrance
1985, Carlo Scarpa

The career of the quixotic twentieth-century Venetian architect Carlo Scarpa can be traced in a day's tour of his native city: the deft installations of artifacts in the Accademia and Museo Correr; the early homage to Frank Lloyd Wright at the Olivetti showroom on the Piazza San Marco and the Venezuela Pavilion on the Biennale grounds; and the liquid material renderings and dense narrative strategies of the Querini-Stampalia Foundation (later deployed on a grander scale at the Brion Family Cemetery not far away in San Vito d'Altivole. A final, often overlooked, chapter in this strange oeuvre is found on the Campo dei Tolentini at the entrance to the Istituto Universitaria di Architettura di Venezia, where Scarpa taught for years. Completed by Sergio Los after Scarpa's untimely death in 1978, the entrance and the garden it shields combine to gently reveal the unsettling, often repressed, undertow of Venice.

Facing the Campo, a massive concrete wall deliberately evokes the plinth of the neighboring church of San Nicolò da Tolentino. The wall, however, eerily flips the steps of San Nicolò to the vertical, and mysteriously supports a hooded canopy through an endless series of concatenations —the canopy itself often cradles giggling schoolchildren (how did they get up there?). Gliding silently on one glimmering Muntz metal roller, the entry gate has an elegant black steel structure with an Istrian stone plaque engraved with Vico's phrase, *verum ipsum factum.*

Yet Venice is the home of strange truths. For passing through the plinth to the netherworld inside, we find ourselves walking in a canal bordered by islands that crest above the entry wall. The islands are articulated as verdant earth (grass), sky (terra-cotta roofing tiles), and water (the ancient sunken aquatic portal). We do not know where we are yet we seem to be hovering, suspended, beyond terra firma. We are in Venice.

MICHAEL CADWELL
Architect

1.2 Santa Maria Gloriosa dei Frari

Campo dei Frari

☎ 041 522 26 37; www.sacred-destinations.com

It really is glorious, with some of the greatest works by Bellini, Titian, Donatello, Paolo da Venezia, and the Vivarini. Donatello's *Saint John the Baptist* was made for his fellow Florentines who maintained a chapel in the Frari. Bellini's triptych in the sacristy was endowed as the altarpiece of the woman buried in the pavement in front of the altar; her son (one of Bellini's patrons) is buried in the grandiose tomb that frames the entrance to the sacristy from the church. Their kinsman was a patron of Titian's Pesaro Altarpiece—Pesaro's tomb is on the wall next to it; and Titian's sublime *Assumption of the Virgin* on the high altar commemorates the dedication of the church. ("Santa Maria Gloriosa" means "Saint Mary assumed into heaven.") Titian himself is believed to have been buried here, and a rather undistinguished neoclassical monument marks the spot; and opposite is the tomb of the heart of the great sculptor Canova (other body parts are in the Accademia and in Possagno, the sculptor's birthplace: a man of parts). While you're at the Frari, you can easily visit the Scuola Grande di San Rocco and its church, which are literally

VENICE

SAN POLO AND SANTA CROCE

1 Istituto Universitaria di Architettura
   di Venezia

2 Santa Maria Gloriosa dei Frari

3 Scuola Grande di San Rocco

4 Scuola Grande di San Giovanni
   Evangelista

5 San Zan Degolà

6 Campiello del Pistor

🍴 7 Osteria Da Fiore

🎁 8 Mascari

🍴 9 Alla Madonna

next door. The Scuola is decorated top to bottom with some of Tintoretto's greatest works.

RONA GOFFEN
The late Rona Goffen was an art historian.

1.3   Scuola Grande di San Rocco

Campo di San Rocco

📞 041 523 48 64; www.scuolagrandesanrocco.it

Paintings
1564–1587, Tintoretto

In Italy there are several storehouses of greatness: buildings that house the most intense production of the works of great masters: these include the Arena Chapel in Padua (Giotto), San Marco in Florence (Fra Angelico), the Sistine Chapel in Rome (Michelangelo), and the Scuola San Rocco in Venice (the treasures of Tintoretto).

Begun around 1517 to honor San Rocco, the saint who ministered to plague victims, the building contains many of the most outstanding works of the painter Jacopo Robusti, known to us as Tintoretto. In 1564, the Confraternity held a competition to decide which artist would be chosen to make the first important painting in the building. Tintoretto, breaking the rules that called for the artists to submit drawings, instead made a painting, installed it, and gave it to the Confraternity. He was then chosen to make all the paintings for the building. Accepting this responsibility gave him the impetus to make his greatest works, and the Scuola contains more than a hundred—some decorative, some mythological, others of the most devout religious passion—but all meant to inform and entice the viewer. In sum, it is one of my favorite places on this earth.

Jean-Paul Sartre's essay entitled "The Prisoner of Venice" has caused me to love Tintoretto even more. It's collected in *Situations I*, a book of his essays.

JACK BEAL
Painter

Annunciations

If Last Suppers are among the special treasures of Florence, the Annunciation is a subject inventively addressed by Venetian artists. Particularly wonderful are those by Titian and Tintoretto in the Scuola di San Rocco, but most startling of all is the explosive apparition that adorns a dark side altar in the church of San Salvatore. Thanks to Titian, the mystery of revelation is made visible. And should you ever find your way to the Cathedral San Pietro in the northern city of Treviso, you will be rewarded by one of Titian's earliest and strangest variants on the theme.

WILLIAM E. WALLACE
Art historian

ITINERARY:
1. San Salvatore, Campo San Salvatore
2. Scuola Grande di San Rocco, Campo di San Rocco

1.4 Scuola Grande di San Giovanni Evangelista
Campiello della Scuola 2454
☎ 041 71 82 34; www.scuolasangiovanni.it

Even if you don't go in, the entranceway is worth the visit—my favorite eagle, in honor of Saint John.

RONA GOFFEN
The late Rona Goffen was an art historian.

1.5 San Zan Degolà (San Giovanni Decollato)
c. 10th century
Campo San Zan Degolà
041 524 0672
Closed Sundays.

Frescoes
c. early 13th century

Outside of Torcello, there are few places in Venice where one can still see the splendid work of medieval fresco artists. Most Venetian churches were long ago assaulted by

the Renaissance or Baroque movement and now stand
dressed up in their finery. To get a glimpse of the medieval
Venetian past in an atmosphere of peace and solitude, head
straight for the church of San Zan Degolà (Saint John the
Baptist Beheaded). The church itself probably dates back
to the tenth century and was beautifully decorated with
frescoes in the early thirteenth century. After that, however,
it fell on a long history of hard times, and the parish itself
was closed in 1810. In 1983, a project to uncover and
restore the medieval frescoes began. It was only in 1994
that the doors were finally opened to the public. This serene
structure still breathes the austerity and religious devotion
of the medieval parish church. Best of all, no one goes
there. You will likely have this jewel to yourself, and you'll
be free to think, pray, or admire the frescoes at your leisure.
Next, walk out into the open campo, at all times devoid of
tourists, where you can drink in the peace and simple
charm that is fast becoming extinct in modern Venice.
THOMAS F. MADDEN
Historian

Santa Croce Walk

The walk from San Zan Degolà to San Giacomo dell'Orio
(a beautiful church and campo) to Campo Sant'Agostin to
San Stin to the Frari: this takes you past the houses of the
great Venetian diarist Marino Sanudo, the greatest-ever
printer Aldus Manutius, and a very beautiful relief attached
to a building as you approach Campo Sant'Agostin.
RONA GOFFEN
The late Rona Goffen was an art historian.

ITINERARY:
1. San Zan Degolà Campo San Zan Degolà
2. San Giacomo dell'Orio Campo San Giacomo dell'Orio
3. Campo Sant'Agostin
4. Campo San Stin
5. Santa Maria Gloriosa dei Frari, Campo dei Frari

1.6 Campiello del Pistor
Begins at Campo Sant'Agostin.

Right-angle intersections are rare in Venice. An approximate example is where the canals of Sant'Agostin, San Stin and San Polo meet. Three of the corners are brick walls, flush on the water, but the fourth is an open *campiello*, a little courtyard. Called Campiello del Pistor (*pistor* is an old Venetian term, via Latin, meaning a bread baker or *fornaio*), this small courtyard offers an intimate sense of how truly this city is a cluster of islands, separated and connected by canals. The only foot access is from Campo Sant'Agostin: Calle del Pistor starts where Calle de la Chiesa and Rio Terrà Secondo meet, then it turns right after a few meters, leading to Corte del Pistor. Here, on the left, the narrow, dark Sottoportego del Pistor—a covered passageway—continues the Calle until it dead-ends in the Campiello. Directly across is Palazzo Donà delle Rose (sixteenth-century, restored early 1800s), today an elementary school. The large palazzo diagonally to the right belonged to the Almateo d'Oderzo family, now extinct, which boasted poets, literary figures, and a famous medical doctor. To the left can be seen a bit of the pink Palazzo Corner Mocenigo's main façade (designed by Michele Sanmicheli and completed in 1564, five years after his death), today the Guardia di Finanza, also visible from Campo San Polo. Just beyond is the cone-shaped top of the Church of San Polo's bell tower.

Of historical interest: a stone plaque on the Gothic palazzo, Rio Terrà Secondo 2311, recalls the printing press of Aldo Manuzio, and around the corner, Ramo Astora 2313, is the site of the home of Daniele Manin, Venice's great leader of the 1848 uprising against the Austrians.

SALLY SPECTOR
Artist

1.7 Osteria Da Fiore

Calle dello Scaleter 2202/a
☎ 041 72 13 08; www.dafiore.net
Closed Sundays and Mondays.

🍴 The place to go for Venice's most exquisite seafood. In
Patricia Wells's list of the world's ten best restaurants that
appeared in the *International Herald Tribune*, Da Fiore
placed fifth. Try lunch if you can't get a table for dinner.
MARCELLA HAZAN
Chef and cookbook author

1.8 Mascari

Ruga dei Spezieri 381, Rialto Market
☎ 041 522 97 62; www.imascari.com
Closed Sundays.

🎁 Finest quality dried porcini; true pine nuts; whole candied
citron; saffron; dried *lamon* beans, the best for making
pasta e fagioli. Mascari also carries a fine variety of
condiments produced with white truffles. If you are
going in the fall, you must take home at least one jar of
mostarda veneta by Lazzari. This quince mustard is a
great specialty from Vicenza. Use it on meats, but most
sublimely, mix it with mascarpone.
MARCELLA HAZAN
Chef and cookbook author

Bacari

The sole aspect of authentically Venetian life that has yet
to be altered by tourism is snacking at a *bacaro*. A *bacaro*
is a small, cheery, crowded food-and-wine bar where,
although tables are available, habitués usually stand by the
counter and consume liberal amounts of young, good wine
by the glass while maintaining sobriety with a variety of
succulent, freshly made tidbits known as *cicheti* (chee-
keyh-tee), the Venetian version of *tapas*. These may include

baccalà whipped to a creamy consistency with olive oil and milk; *folpeti*, tender braised baby octopus; sardines in *saor*; baked eggplant; artichoke bottoms; risotto with cuttlefish ink; *soppressa*—the indigenous soft Venetian salami; thick, hand-sliced prosciutto; *musetto*—the Venetian version of *cotechino*, an incredibly tender, cooked salami; *polpette*, little meatballs; spiced sliced tongue; *nervetti*—boiled, tenderly chewy bits of calf's feet served with olive oil, parsley, and sliced raw onion; and *tramezzini*, the Venetian sandwich that encloses between small triangles of soft bread an infinite variety of stuffings, often laced with mayonnaise. Not every *bacaro* has all of these choices; the assortment varies from place to place and each has some specialty it does better than anyone else. The visitor endowed with gastronomic curiosity and an unbiased palate will nowhere in Italy spend a more savory and convivial hour or two than in a Venetian *bacaro*. Most *bacari* open early in the morning, close for three hours or so in the afternoon, and reopen for what is usually a short evening, some closing as early as 8:30 p.m. There are exceptions, however. There are a dozen or more *bacari* in every neighborhood. These are some of our favorites:

Osteria da Alberto

Calle larga Giacinto Gallina, Castello 5401; ☎041 523 81 53
Closed Sundays.

🍴 Alberto sold his immensely popular *osteria* in 1977, but Marco and Andrea, his successors, have not disappointed. Good variety of simple wines by the glass.

Antico Dolo

Ruga Rialto, San Polo 778
☎041 522 65 46; www.anticodolo.it
Closed Sundays.

🍴 One of the oldest and most atmosphere-laden *bacari*. Stays open until 11 p.m. or later, depending on business, and serves good hot food at table.

Do Mori
Calle dei do Mori, San Polo 429; ☎ 041 522 54 01
Closed Sundays.

🍴 It is Venice's most celebrated *bacaro*, famous for its ambience, an admirable selection of superb red wines available by the glass, and exquisite little toasted sandwiches stuffed with truffles or goose breast or topped with *musetto*. It, too, has recently changed hands and we have yet to try it under its new management. Stand-up service only.
MARCELLA HAZAN
Chef and cookbook author

1.9 ### Alla Madonna
Calle della Madonna 594, Rialto Market
☎ 041 522 38 24; www.ristoranteallamadonna.com
Closed Wednesdays. Closed in January and two weeks in August.

🍴 A large, lively, busy place, popular for decades for its reliable cooking and affable but rather brisk service. We prefer more intimate surroundings and a kitchen that is geared to a small production, but the restaurant can nonetheless be recommended for consistently good fish.
MARCELLA HAZAN
Chef and cookbook author

Canals

By any means possible try to come by a boat and have someone row you, or row yourself, through the quiet, out-of-the-way canals in the dead of night. It is a magical mode of time travel through eons of literature and imagination. Getting lost remains the best possible way to see Venice.
SUSAN KLEINBERG
Artist

CANNAREGIO

2.1 **San Giobbe**
Campo San Giobbe
☎ 041 275 04 62
Closed Sundays.

San Giobbe is well worth a visit, especially for its beautiful decorative reliefs by the Lombardo in the chancel, the Della Robbia–style chapel in the left aisle (a Florentine interloper in a very Venetian church), and the Savoldo in the sacristy.
RONA GOFFEN
The late Rona Goffen was an art historian.

2.2 **Sant'Alvise**
Campo di Sant'Alvise

Among the plethora of things that pack this picturesque, medieval church, there are three spectacularly great Tiepolos—the *Way to Calvary, Christ Crowned with Thorns*, the *Flagellation*—that look ahead to Delacroix. The church is not open on a regular basis, so you should check hours before you trek out to it.
KEITH CHRISTIANSEN
Chairman of the Department of European Paintings at the Metropolitan Museum of Art

Food Shopping

🎁 Food shops are open from 9 a.m. to 1 p.m., and 5 p.m. to 7:30 p.m.; on Wednesdays they open only in the morning; on Sundays they are closed all day. Other shops stay open from 9 a.m. to 12:30 p.m., and 3:30 p.m. to 7 p.m., and those that cater to the tourist trade even stay open on Sunday.
MARCELLA HAZAN
Chef and cookbook author

The Venice Ghetto

An absolute must is to walk very long and very far and get as lost (and as removed from the crowded strip between San Marco and the Rialto) as is humanly possible. This strategy is likely to bring you, sooner or later, to the ghetto, where a tour of the synagogues—a must for any Jew—is an interesting experience for anyone; there's nothing quite like them anywhere in the world. On my last visit, I eavesdropped on a priest from Vicenza who was taking his parishioners on a tour; in the museum, he made a special point of showing them my own two favorite items: two remarkable embroidered ark curtains, one representing the gift of manna in the desert and the other depicting the Waters of Salvation [Isaiah 12.2–3] engulfing Jerusalem, making it look remarkably like Venice.

JACQUELINE OSHEROW
Poet

2.3 ## Madonna dell'Orto
15th century
Campo Madonna dell'Orto

Saint John the Baptist and Four Saints
c. 1493, Cima da Conegliano

Adoration of the Golden Calf and The Last Judgment
1562–1564, Tintoretto

Venice is an endless discovery, and there is scarcely a church that does not give pleasure for either its site, architecture, paintings, or the effect of accumulation. The walk to Madonna dell'Orto, occasionally referred to as Santa Maria dell'Orto, will introduce you to an altogether quieter Venice than the area around San Marco. It takes you through the ghetto to a workers' quarter that was the parish of Tintoretto, whose father was a dyer. The large, airy church is fifteenth-century Gothic with a fine, flamboyant entrance door. Immediately to the right, upon entering, is a hauntingly beautiful altarpiece by Cima da Conegliano of Saint John the Baptist. It's in its original frame. Tintoretto is buried in the apse, which is in all respects a monument to his ambitions and achievement. The lateral walls are filled with two spectacular and enormous canvases—Tintoretto's response to Michelangelo's *Last Judgment* in the Sistine Chapel. One shows the *Adoration of the Golden Calf*, the other his own vision of *The Last Judgment*. The first contrasts an aristocratic picnic in the lower half to a vertiginously placed Moses receiving the tablets of the Ten Commandments from a God the Father who seems, literally, to swim through the heavens accompanied by wingless angels. *The Last Judgment* is an over-the-top and spell-binding cataclysm. This is pictorial rhetoric at its most hypnotic. You will either be swept up in the movement (correct response) or turn away disappointed at the lack of interest in individual psychology (wrong response). The spandrels of the apse are filled with images of Temperance, Justice, Prudence, and Strength, and there are two other large canvases, the *Vision of Saint Peter of the Cross* and the *Martyrdom of Saint Paul*—also Tintoretto. Over the door to the sacristy is another beautiful large canvas by Tintoretto of the Presentation of the Virgin in the Temple that scintillates in the afternoon light, and in the aisle on the opposite side of the church is an altarpiece showing Saint Agnes resuscitating a youth. Another altar used to have a lovely painting of the Madonna and Child by Bellini. It was stolen a few years back and as of this time has not been retrieved.

KEITH CHRISTIANSEN
Chairman of the Department of European Paintings at the Metropolitan Museum of Art

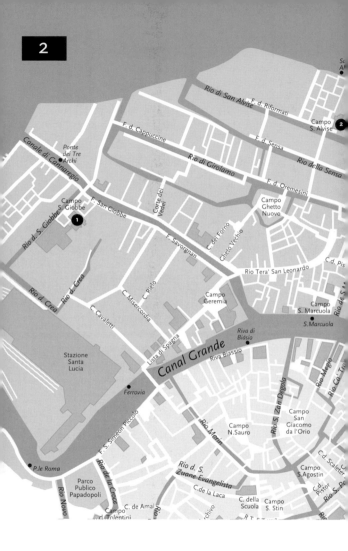

2

Rio di San Alvise

F. d. Riformati

Campo
S. Alvise

Canale di Cannaregio

F. d. Cappuccine

Ponte
dei Tre
Archi

Rio di Girolama

F. d. Sensa

Rio della Sensa

F. d. Oremesini

Campo
S. Giobbe

F. San Giobbe

Corte dei
Vedei

Campo
Ghetto
Nuovo

C. dei Forno

Gheto Vechio

F. Savorgnan

C.d. Pis

Rio d. S. Giobbe

Rio Tera' San Leonardo

Rio d. Crea

Rio d. Crea

C. Riefo

C. Misericordia

Campo
Geremia

Campo
S. Marcuola

C.d. S.

C. Cavaletti

S. Marcuola

Lista di Spagna

Riva di
Biasio

Stazione
Santa
Lucia

Canal Grande

Riva Biassio

Ferrovia

Rio S. Zan Degola

Rio Megio

Rio Ca' Trov

Campo
N.Sauro

Campo
San
Giacomo
da l'Orio

C.d. Scaleter

P.le Roma

Rio Marin

Campo
S.Agostin

C.d.
Pistor

Rio d. S.
Zuane Evangelista

Rio d. la Croce

C.de la Laca

Rio S. Pe

Parco
Publico
Papadopoli

C. de Amai

C. della
Scuola

Campo
S. Stin

Rio Novo

Campo
d. Tolentini

chivo

CANNAREGIO

1 San Giobbe
2 Sant'Alvise
3 Madonna dell'Orto
4 Scuola Nuova Della Misericordia
5 Gesuiti
6 Tuttocasa

7 Fiaschetteria Toscana
8 San Giovanni Crisostomo
9 Pastificio Giacomo Rizzo
10 La Colonna
11 Santa Maria dei Miracoli

2.4 Scuola Nuova Della Misericordia
Begun c. 1532, Jacopo Sansovino
Fondamenta della Misericordia 3599

The largest hall of an existing fraternity *scuola*, built according to a Sansovino design but never completed. Formerly used as a basketball court, notwithstanding its sixteenth-century frescoes.
GIANFRANCO MOSSETTO
Merchant banker

2.5 Gesuiti
Campo dei Gesuiti

The tiled floor rolls as if the sea itself shaped it. It's quiet, ancient, private, and idiosyncratic.
SUSAN KLEINBERG
Artist

Vaporetto Ride

My favorite thing to do in Venice—aside, perhaps from going to see the Carpaccios in the Scuola di San Giorgio degli Schiavoni—is to go to Piazzale Roma and get a seat outside in the front of the slower-than-slow no. 1 vaporetto, which makes every stop on the Grand Canal. This ride is a pleasure at any time of day, though it's perhaps especially lovely at dusk.
JACQUELINE OSHEROW
Poet

2.6 Tuttocasa
Campo la Santi Apostoli 4518; ☎041 523 85 85

🎁 A very well stocked neighborhood kitchen and housewares shop near the Strada Nuova thoroughfare. A good place to go for two of those items indispensable to Marcella's

kitchen: *retine*, wire net flame spreaders for gas burners, and peelers. They have a nice assortment of handsomely designed Italian Lucite and brightly colored plastic ware.
MARCELLA HAZAN
Chef and cookbook author

2.7   **Fiaschetteria Toscana**
San Giovanni Grisostomo 5719
☎ 041 528 52 81; www.fiaschetteriatoscana.it
Closed Tuesdays, and Wednesdays for lunch.

🍴 Despite the name, it has been an authentically Venetian restaurant for decades, with a varied menu that includes some meat but specializes in fish. Their signature dish is *Fritto della Serenissima*, a perfectly fried mixture of seafood and vegetables. If you like white truffles, ask for their *tagliolini coi tartufi*. Excellent wine list. Try for Roberto or Claudio as your waiter, and leave room for one of Mariuccia's own desserts.
MARCELLA HAZAN
Chef and cookbook author

2.8   **San Giovanni Crisostomo**
1497–1504, Mauro Coducci
Campo San Giovanni Crisostomo

A beautiful building by Mauro Coducci, his last work, with one of Bellini's last works, the *Saints Jerome, Christopher and Louis of Toulouse*, dated 1513. Opposite this, a relief altarpiece by Tullio Lombardo of the *Coronation of the Virgin*, neoclassical in style avant la lettre. On the high altar, a great early work by Sebastiano Veneziano (before he got his papal title *del Piombo*), representing the titular saint with three lovely female saints.
RONA GOFFEN
The late Rona Goffen was an art historian.

Cannaregio to San Marco

When I found myself crossing Rio San Giovanni Crisostomo in the Cannaregio section of Venice, I knew I had crossed the bridge from west to east. Saint John Chrysostom, whose liturgy continues to be used in Eastern Christian churches today, was once Patriarch of Constantinople. And no sooner had I entered Saint Mark's Basilica than I felt transported to Byzantium. At Saint Mark's one is completely and warmly enveloped in icon-like mosaics, all depicting the great stories and saints from the Old and New Testaments on glistening gold backgrounds.

MARY ANN HAICK DINAPOLI
Historian and genealogist

2.9 Pastificio Giacomo Rizzo
San Giovanni Crisostomo 5778, ☎ 041 522 28 24

🎁 Balsamic vinegar; white truffle paste; olive oil (ask to see the Lake Garda oil from the Riviera Bresciana). All their best products are on display in the window, with their respective prices, so you can browse and decide what to ask before going in.

MARCELLA HAZAN
Chef and cookbook author

An Enchanted Evening
Board no. 1 boat at San Marcuola to San Zaccaria
Board no. 82 for return to San Marcuola

I take my favorite guests for an enchanting nighttime boat ride down the Grand Canal on the vaporetto, the public water bus. Armed with luscious *gelati* from Il Gelatone (Rio Terrà della Maddalena, Cannaregio 2063, ☎ 041 72 06 31—near the Casinò on Strada Nova), we board the no. 1 boat at San Marcuola and try to score a seat out front, where there's nothing between us and the dark water.

We cruise past magical palaces and under the Rialto and Accademia bridges to magnificent Saint Mark's. Disembarking at San Zaccaria, we cross the nearby bridge for the landing stage for line no. 82 (the one via San Giorgio, not Rialto). This transports us via the broad Giudecca Canal and then the vast silent port precincts, eventually looping back to the railway station and San Marcuola.

GILLIAN PRICE
Travel writer

2.10 La Colonna

Fondamenta Nuove 5329, near Calle del Fumo
☎ 041 522 96 41
Closed Sunday evenings and Mondays.

When Bruno Paolato was a partner chef in Ai Mercanti (San Polo 1588, ☎ 041 524 22 82), that establishment was one of our favorite hangouts. Bruno fell out with his partners and ensconced himself in this small, charming trattoria. It has tables for outdoor dining in clement weather and it is happily off the tracks that tourists usually beat.

MARCELLA HAZAN
Chef and cookbook author

2.11 Santa Maria dei Miracoli

c. 1481–1489, Pietro Lombardo with his sons, Tullio and Antonio
Campo dei Miracoli
☎ 041 275 04 62; www.sacred-destinations.com
Closed Sundays.

Perhaps the most beautiful little church in Venice, if not in all Italy, this is a favorite church of Venetian brides. From 1988 to 1998, Save Venice restored the entire church and everything in it. To my knowledge, it is the only Italian church in such pristine condition.

BEATRICE H. GUTHRIE
Former director of Save Venice

CASTELLO

3.1 **Colonna**
Calle della Fava 5595; ☎ 041 528 51 37
Closed Sundays.

🎁 A wine shop with a very fine assortment of grappas. Also
carries one or two good olive oils.
MARCELLA HAZAN
Chef and cookbook author

3.2 **Didovich**
Campo Santa Marina 5987/a; ☎ 041 523 91 81
Closed Sundays.

🍴 If you are on the way to visit the great church of Santi
Giovanni e Paolo and its monumental campo with the
celebrated equestrian statue of Bartolomeo Colleoni, stop
at Didovich in Campo Santa Marina. They also make
Venice's tastiest *salatini*, little vegetable tarts.
MARCELLA HAZAN
Chef and cookbook author

3.3 **Scuola Grande di San Marco**
Campo Santi Giovanni e Paolo

Façade
*1487–1490, Pietro Lombardo and sons and Giovanni Buori
Completed 1495 by Mauro Coducci*

A piazza with a most unusual architectural façade in perspective reliefs. Located next to the side canal, the building
façade was designed to relate to the viewer approaching
the space. Each elevation and section is revealed as one
moves forward and turns the corner.
JOHN L. WONG
Landscape architect

3.4 Monument to Bartolomeo Colleoni
1481–1488, Andrea del Verrocchio
Campo di Santi Giovanni e Paolo

One of the greatest equestrian monuments stands in the Campo di Santi Giovanni e Paolo: Verrocchio's *Colleoni*. A *condottiere* who had served the Venetian Republic, Colleoni provided funds in his will for the monument to be made and erected in the Piazza di San Marco, the ducal basilica. (There is only one piazza in Venice; every other square is a campo.) Such a site was of course unthinkable for the Venetians, who willfully misinterpreted the testamentary bequest to refer to the campo in front of the Scuola or Confraternity of Saint Mark—that is, the Campo di Santi Giovanni e Paolo. (The *scuola* is now the Civic Hospital, and you don't want to go there.)

Because Colleoni's name sounds like the Italian word *coglioni*—cullions or testicles—he used them as an emblem; this kind of crude punning is typical of Renaissance humor. (I think it's funny, too.) The *coglioni* are represented throughout the statue and its base, looking like plump quotation marks.

Rona Goffen
The late Rona Goffen was an art historian.

3.5 Santi Giovanni e Paolo (San Zanipolo)
Campo Santi Giovanni e Paolo
041 523 59 13; www.basilicasantigiovanniepaolo.it

Not the easiest place to find in the labyrinthine alleys of Venezia, the Church of Santi Giovanni e Paolo is on the western border of the Castello district, away from the well-worn paths around the Piazza San Marco and the Rialto Bridge. Beyond the lovely square of the Campo Santa Maria Formosa, wend your way through narrow *calli* in a generally northern direction and you will emerge into an airy square with a magisterial equestrian statue, the Colleoni

3

Campiello
Widmann

Campo
d. Miracoli

③
④
⑤

Campo
S.S. Giovani
e Paolo

C. d. Teatro

Rio d. S. Marina

Campo
Marina

②

Barbaria de le Tole

Rio S. Giovanni

C. d.
Fava

Rio d. Pestrin

Rialto

Campo
S.Maria
Formosa

⑦

①

Szda. S.Lio

C. I. S.Lorenzo

Campo
S.Lorenzo

Campo
della Fava

C. d. Mondo
Nuovo

⑥

⑧

Rio d. Spezia

Rio de S. Zulian

C. al Ponte
della Guerra

⑨

Rio Fontana

Rio d. S. Lorenzo

Rio d. Mondo

C. Querini

C. Fiubera

C. larga S. Marco

Rio d. Palazzo

C. Sz. Zorzi

Rio d. S. Provolo

Rio d. Greci

Riva d.

Piazza
San
Marco

F. S.Apollonia

⑩

Rio di Vin

Campo
S.Zaccaria

⑪

Riva degli Schiavoni

San
Zaccaria
Danieli

San
Zaccaria
Jolanda

Mo. Vittorio
Emanuele

Riva
segli
Schiavoni

Molo S.Marco

San Marco
Giardinetti

San Marco
Vallaresco

Riva de

Punta
Dogana

Canale Di San Marco

Campo
San Giorgio
Maggiore

Darsena

San Giorgio Maggiore

CASTELLO

🍴 1 Colonna

🍷 2 Didovich

3 Scuola Grande di San Marco

4 Monument to Bartolomeo Colleoni

5 Santi Giovanni e Paolo
   (San Zanipolo)

🍷 6 Alle Testiere

🍷 7 Al Mascaron

8 Santa Maria Formosa

9 Fondazione Querini Stampalia

10 Sant'Apollonia

11 San Zaccaria

12 Scuola di San Giorgio degli
    Schiavoni

13 San Francesco della Vigna

🍴🍷 14 Ristorante Al Covo

15 Arsenale

memorial of Andrea Verrocchio. Looming over the campo is the church of San Zanipolo, the Venetian name for the sanctuary dedicated to two minor fourth-century saints. The church is a magnificent Venetian Gothic structure where, as opposed to so many other sites, no admission is charged and where seventy tourists aren't jostling one another to glimpse a rare Titian altarpiece.

Great Gothic churches are designed to make man feel insignificant and reverential in the presence of divine power. As large as San Zanipolo appears from the exterior, the first-time visitor is unprepared for the cavernous space that welcomes you upon entering the front door. The interior is somewhat dark, with the hushed murmur of a few people milling about while monks float by in their cassocks, a reminder of the church's important Dominican traditions. Besides the overwhelming size of the church, why should a visitor to Venezia spend the time to seek out this remote place? It isn't the best place to see paintings by renowned Renaissance masters—Bellini, Titian, and Tintoretto are better represented elsewhere. Nor is it the place to admire a Veronese or Tiepolo ceiling fresco. No, come to San Zanipolo to see the finest survey of Venetian sculpture, from the austerity of the Gothic to the exuberance of the Baroque. The vast interior of San Zanipolo is the greatest repository of ducal funerary monuments in Venice. The tombs provide a valuable overview of the stylistic development of Venetian art. More important, they provide an unparalleled insight into the power and personalities of the Doges themselves, far more so than the sterile reception rooms of the Palazzo Ducale. Come to see the monuments, come to contemplate the lives of the powerful rulers of the Republic, come to experience the wavy, buckled mosaic pavement, but do not come in shorts or a tank top, or one of those apparently serene and imperturbable monks will promptly and unceremoniously escort you to the door.

EMILIE K. JOHNSON
Ph.D. candidate in art and architectural history

I particularly like Lotto's *Saint Antoninus* and the great
ducal tombs by the Lombardo and others. Outside, at the
east end of the church (in back of the apse), is the site of
the Bellini family graves; Gentile and Giovanni were
buried there.

RONA GOFFEN
The late Rona Goffen was an art historian.

Capella del Rosario
Ceiling paintings by Veronese

Long ago, I discovered a Veronese ceiling in the side chapel
(to the left, coming from the back entrance) and became
fascinated with its complexity and lack of predictability.
Gazing up, there is a sense of what it means to separate
from the terrestrial.

SUSAN KLEINBERG
Artist

Tomb of Alvise Diedo
Pietro Lombardo

In San Zanipolo, don't miss the magnificent floor tomb
just outside the Chapel of the Madonna della Pace. Carved
by Pietro Lombardo, this tomb is a late-fifteenth-century
example of *niello* decoration, a sumptuous technique that
involves filling in the incised lines of the marble with
nigellum, a mixture of copper, sulfur, lead, and silver. The
amount of luxurious detail, contrasting the dark inlaid
lines with the radiant Istrian marble, is a measure of the
astounding skill and sensibilities of Renaissance Venetian
artists. Only with difficulty can we reconstruct the original
stunning appearance of the slab before it was worn smooth
by the innumerable footsteps of generations. Lorenzetti, the
standard authority on Venetian buildings and their con-
tents, writes of this small monument using the word *ele-
gantissima*, and describes the memorial as *squisita arte*

quattrocentesca—exquisite fifteenth-century art. English offers nothing more precise to capture it.

EMILIE K. JOHNSON
Ph.D. candidate in art and architectural history

3.6 Alle Testiere

Calle del Mondo Nuovo 5801
☎ 041 522 72 20; www.osterialletestiere.it
Closed Sundays.

🍴 You can get some of the tastiest cooking in Venice at this miniature, twenty-seat restaurant. Bruno, the owner-chef, trained at the legendary Corte Sconta (Calle del Pestrin 3886, ☎ 522 70 24) in the bygone days when it was Venice's most glorious trattoria. Contact Luca, the partner who attends to the dining room.

MARCELLA HAZAN
Chef and cookbook author

3.7 Al Mascaron

Calle Lunga Santa Maria Formosa 5225
☎ 041 522 59 95; www.osteriamascaron.it
Closed Sundays.

🍴 Offers some of the best food served by a casual trattoria in Venice. Excellent wines. Very popular, very busy, long waits are common.

MARCELLA HAZAN
Chef and cookbook author

3.8 Santa Maria Formosa

Campo Santa Maria Formosa
☎ 041 275 04 62

Saint Barbara Altarpiece
Early 16th century, Palma Vecchio

Madonna della Misericordia
1473, Bartolomeo Vivarini

Another of these two-main-entrance churches is Santa Maria Formosa, literally, "Shapely Virgin Mary," built, according to legend, by a monk inspired by a dream of the Madonna. (You find this kind of delicious information in Tassini's *Curiosità Veneziane*.) The Formosa has one of Palma Vecchio's most beautiful works, the Saint Barbara altarpiece, and one of Bartolomeo Vivarini's best, a triptych of the *Madonna della Misericordia*.

RONA GOFFEN

The late Rona Goffen was an art historian.

3.9 Fondazione Querini Stampalia

Calle Querini 4778

☎ 041 271 14 11; www.querinistampalia.it

Closed Mondays.

Ground floor

1959–1963, Carlo Scarpa

In the fall and winter seasons, a delightfully warming experience is to visit La Biblioteca Querini Stampalia, open until midnight, according to the stipulation of Conte Giovanni Querini Stampalia, who made the city a gift of his ancestral palazzo and library in 1869. A modern Venetian architect, Carlo Scarpa, designed elements of a purely Venetian palazzo including a private bridge, a water entry, and a garden, in a modern idiom of exquisite and understated beauty.

MARGARET SPENCER MATZ

Architect

3.10 Sant'Apollonia

Fondamenta Sant'Apollonia 4312

☎ 055 238 86 07

Closed the first, third, and fifth Sunday, and second and fourth Monday of every month.

Cloister

12th century

It's late in the morning and you're heading for the Piazza
San Marco. You've survived the natives vying for *scampi*
at the Rialto markets, outmaneuvered the crowds buying
Murano glass on the Rialto Bridge, and sidestepped the
throngs milling around the McDonald's in the Campo San
Bartolomeo. You've negotiated the claustrophobic ravine
of the Merceria, stuttering along nose-to-tail in this
seething shopping artery connecting the Rialto to the
Piazza. You enter the great square under the arch of the
Clock Tower only to face a sea of humanity more intimi-
dating than any *acqua alta*—tides of polyglot tour groups
flood the Piazza, the Piazzetta, and the Riva beyond.
Magari! The arcades are inundated with shoppers clutching
Gucci shoes, Fendi handbags, and Hermès scarves. Lines of
tourists snake out from the Basilica, the Palazzo Ducale,
and the Campanile. Instigated by miscreants feeding them
corn, the infamous pigeons of San Marco are rehearsing a
nightmarish scene from a Hitchcock film. The world closes
in on you and you start to feel faint. It's too early for alco-
hol, and you remember that you don't smoke. *Ma che!*

A sanctuary is not far off. Quell your panic and set
off through the Piazzetta dei Leoncini (the little square of
the lions) adjacent to San Marco. Walk around behind
the Basilica, carefully avoiding the first bridge encountered,
which, in a marketing stroke of genius, dead-ends at a
glass factory sales outlet. Turn right, then left across
a small bridge, and right again onto the Rughetta
Sant'Apollonia to a sign marked Museo Diocesano. Go
through the portal, but not to the museum, a second-story
clutter of mundane bits salvaged from deconsecrated
churches. Your destination is the lovely cloister of
Sant'Apollonia that houses the museum's entrance. The
twelfth-century structure is the sole remaining example of
a Romanesque cloister in Venice. Sit quietly amid the

slender double columns and the ancient wellhead, or read beneath the small semicircular arches that encircle the worn bricks of the pavement. A sense of calm pervades the cloister, long associated with a Benedictine Abbey close to Torcello. After a time, when you are refreshed, recovered from the frenetic pace outside, you can return to the sights of the Piazza, or continue along the route to the nearby church of San Zaccaria to see the finest Giovanni Bellini (signed and dated 1505) in situ.

ERIC DENKER
Art historian

3.11 San Zaccaria

1444–1515; begun by Antonio Gambello and completed by Mauro Codussi
Campo san Zaccaria
☏ 041 522 12 57

Madonna and Four Saints
1505, Giovanni Bellini

The vaporetto ride from San Marco to San Zaccaria must be the most spectacular single bus stop ride in the world. And then, after you return to dry land, you need only to wander through a short alleyway to emerge into a little campo in front of one of the glories of Venetian architecture and art, San Zaccaria. This was the doges' own church before San Marco was built, and the crypt holds the oldest tombs of doges in Venice. But the most dazzling of its attractions is the stunning Bellini altarpiece halfway up the nave. It was one of the treasures Napoleon took back to Paris; a memento of his theft remains, in the piece cut off the top so that the altarpiece would fit the location Napoleon chose for it. Stand in front of the painting when the sun is quite high in the afternoon and you will see the genius of the location as well as the painting. Only one ray of the sun can enter the church through the clerestory windows across the nave, but as the sun moves the ray picks out each of the stunning robes of the saints and the Madonna in turn. The colors glow in succession, creating a magical theater of motion, art, and devout spirituality, all fused into one by the power of both Bellini and San Zaccaria.

THEODORE K. RABB
Historian

Cappella di San Tarasio

Aside from Bellini's ravishing masterpiece, there's also the adjacent Cappella di San Tarasio, which you enter through the sacristy. It has a frescoed vault by Andrea del Castagno, painted with the assistance of Domenico Veneziano in 1442, and splendid triptychs by the Vivarini, with their original carved and gilded frames.

RONA GOFFEN
The late Rona Goffen was an art historian.

Reliefs

Remember to look up in Venice, because there are many wonderful reliefs attached to buildings, sometimes seemingly at random. For example (though not at random), the relief of *putti* with a coat of arms labeling the entrance to the Corte dele Pizzocare; or the relief over the entrance to the Campo di San Zaccaria.

RONA GOFFEN
The late Rona Goffen was an art historian.

3.12 Scuola di San Giorgio degli Schiavoni
Calle Furlani
☎ 041 522 88 28

Saint George and the Dragon
1509–1511, Vittore Carpaccio

One of the often missed artistic jewels in Venice is a cycle of paintings executed by Vittore Carpaccio in 1509–1511 for the Scuola di San Giorgio degli Schiavoni, in the *ses-tiere* of Castello. A *scuola* was not a "school" but a broth-erhood dedicated to the civic good and to performing such acts as visiting the sick, burying the dead, and providing for the material needs of less fortunate members. Many of the more than one hundred *scuole* in Venice also acted as patrons of the arts, commissioning painters to embellish their meeting houses. The Scuola di San Giorgio degli Schiavoni is an example, precious because it is the earliest *scuola* in Venice to retain its original decoration.

We enter the *scuola* building by pushing aside a velvet door-hanging that shuts out virtually all of the Mediter-ranean sun. Inside, the room is dark, and the paintings become our substitute for the glow of the outside world. But what a fantastical other world they conjure! Direct your eyes to the large painting to the left of the doorway, depicting *Saint George Fighting the Dragon*. The members of this brotherhood were immigrants from Dalmatia (on the opposite coast of the Adriatic Sea from Venice), and the painting depicts one of their heroic patron saints fighting for the life of a frightened princess in distant Libya.

Carpaccio, however, had never traveled to such an exotic place as Libya, and instead, he had to rely on his imagination to convincingly render the scene. Resource-fully, he looked at cheap woodblock prints of faraway architecture then circulating among the curious-minded in Venice. The imposing gateway on the distant shoreline to the left, for example, recalls an actual gate in the city of Cairo.

But the foreground scene is pure fantasy, and the artist has let his imagination run unanchored. Parts of dismem-bered bodies, animal skulls, and lizards litter the desert landscape. Saint George spears the winged dragon right through the mouth, and blood pours down its breast. To the right, the princess clasps her hands in gratitude. We witness an exotic tale of carnage, but ultimately of saintly triumph over fear and evil. Inspiration, no doubt, to the

more modestly heroic acts of this Dalmatian brotherhood in their new homeland of Venice.
BARBARA LYNN-DAVIS
Art historian and writer

3.13 San Francesco della Vigna

1534–1554, Jacopo Sansovino; 1562–1572, Andrea Palladio (façade)
Campo San Francesco
☎ 041 520 61 02

Madonna and Child Enthroned

c. 1450, Antonio da Negroponte

This church has the only known work by Antonio da Negroponte, *Madonna and Child Enthroned*, circa 1450, an international Gothic extravaganza. The Giustinian chapel is decorated with elegant reliefs by the Lombardo.
RONA GOFFEN
The late Rona Goffen was an art historian.

Badoer-Giustinian Chapel

15th century, Pietro Lombardi and his school

Don't miss the chapel of the Badoer-Giustinian family, to the left of an altar by members of the Lombardo family.
BEATRICE H. GUTHRIE
Former director of Save Venice

3.14 Ristorante Al Covo

Campiello della Pescaria 3968
☎ 041 522 38 12; www.ristorantealcovo.com
Closed Wednesdays and Thursdays.

Al Covo, by the side of Hotel Gabrielli, is one of the best in Venice. The owner's wife is Texan, his cooking Venetian.
JOHN JULIUS NORWICH
Historian

3.15 Arsenale
Campo Arsenale

Lions

So few visitors wander on foot to the Arsenal (briefly
glimpsed from the vaporetto on its way to the Fondamenta Nuove) that you can inspect undisturbed the lions
that guard its gate. Two were brought as spoils of war
from Piraeus in 1692, and one of these (the farthest to
the left) carries a runic inscription dating to the late
eleventh century, when the Varangian guards (ultimately
of Viking origin) came to Athens from Byzantium. The
inscription, however cryptic, communicates an instant
appreciation of the network of travel for man and beast
in medieval Europe, and the fortunes of war. Even more
moving is a lion closer to the canal, whose archaic sharp-
edged spine will be recognized by anyone who has seen its
fellows on the Terrace of the Lions on Delos. Brought here
in 1718 from Corfu, it, too, conveys its message of exile
and melancholy.

HELEN F. NORTH
Classicist

SAN MARCO

4.1 ### Corte del Duca Sforza

From the Palazzo Grassi, go around the church of San Samuele and head south on Calle Malipiero, then right at Ramo Corte Teatro a few paces until you reach the Corte Sforza.

If you do not have access to a palazzo along the Grand Canal, but you want to enjoy sitting on its banks, relaxing while you watch boatloads of tourists go by and looking like you belong there, then head for the little-visited Corte del Duca Sforza. It is just north of Ca' del Duca, a short walk from the Palazzo Grassi. The Corte is now just an open area in a relatively quiet residential district. Walk through the Corte until you reach an entryway that leads to the Grand Canal itself. There you will find classical white steps descending to the waterway, where you can sit, relax, and soak it all in. When the tourists point to you and take your picture, do your best to look like a Venetian.
THOMAS F. MADDEN
Historian

4.2 ### Save Venice Treasure Hunt

San Marco 2888A

☏ 041 528 52 47; www.savevenice.org
Adjacent to the Ponte dell'Accademia on the San Marco side

Stop by the office of Save Venice and pick up a treasure hunt containing six walks, one for each *sestiere*, or section, of Venice. Prepared with the help of noted author and lecturer John Julius Norwich, the walks and map guide you on a search for each *sestiere*'s artistic and historic highlights. This is a great way to enjoy the prettiest walks in the city. Each section takes about ninety minutes to complete. My favorites are Cannaregio and Santa Croce—parts of town no one ever sees.
BEATRICE H. GUTHRIE
Former director of Save Venice

`4.3` Rigattieri

San Marco 3532
Near Santo Stefano
℡ 041 523 10 81; www.rigattieri-venice.it

An extraordinary assortment of large serving platters and
other modern ceramics.
MARCELLA HAZAN
Chef and cookbook author

`4.4` Museo Fortuny

Palazzo Pesaro, Campo San Benedetto 3780
℡ 848 08 20 00; www.museiciviciveneziani.it
Closed Tuesdays.

Palazzo Fortuny used to be one of the palaces of the Pesaro
family, patrons of Bellini and Titian. It now houses the
Fortuny Museum. (Mariano Fortuny was the textile maker
and designer, to whom one is particularly grateful for ravishing pleated silks.)
RONA GOFFEN
The late Rona Goffen was an art historian.

Traghetti

The *traghetti*, beat-up gondolas that are a substitute for
the vaporetti if you only want to cross the canal, are a
well-kept secret in Venice and generally used only by
locals. (It is considered effete to sit down in one.) One of
my indelible memories of Venice is seeing a gondolier in
full dress uniform casually operating his gondola with one
hand while using a cellular phone with the other.
PAUL PASCAL
Classicist

4.5 Acqua Pazza

Campo Sant'Angelo 3808
☎ 041 277 06 88; www.venicemasaniello.com
Closed Mondays.

🍴 The newest and best pizzeria in town. The staff and owners are from Salerno, a good place to be from if you are making pizza. The pizza is thin and large, the mozzarella is *bufala*, the tomatoes are fresh cherry tomatoes, the oil is extra virgin, and the oven is brick. If you like chili, ask for *olio al peperoncino* that you can dispense to taste at the table. Should they put a bottle of their homemade *limoncello* on your table at the end of the meal, don't fail to fill your glass.

MARCELLA HAZAN
Chef and cookbook author

4.6 Galleria Luce

Campiello della Fenice 1922
☎ 041 522 29 49; www.gallerialuce.com

Located on a corner in the Campiello della Fenice, practically next door to the work-in-progress Teatro La Fenice and the quintessentially charming Hotel La Fenice et des Artistes (Campiello della Fenice 1936, ☎ 041 523 23 33; www.fenicehotels.com), is the Galleria Luce dell'Arte Moderna, a small gem of a gallery where works of *arte moderna* are exhibited. The stars here are Arman, Lucio Fontana and Giorgio De Chirico, but the gallery also displays quality works by lesser-known Italian and international contemporary artists. Renato Luce, who speaks fluent English, established the gallery in 1983, and it is definitely worth stopping by. One never knows what discovery one might make here—Luce has an excellent eye.

NICHOLAS ARCOMANO
Attorney

Walks

After a meal of fish and white wine, there is little that is as satisfying as a stroll among the dark and indistinctly lit *calli* and *campi* of Venice. Footsteps ring on dampened stones; light falls from warm rooms above. Occasionally one comes across a fellow traveler, usually walking more purposefully toward an unknown destination. I have memories of footsteps approaching and fading, a sound isolated by stone and then hushed by gently lapping water. Maybe one hears the splash of a gondola plying the dark waters of back canals. A bridge offers a brief glimpse of where one is and where one might go. But will you be able to get there? It hardly matters, for Venice is perhaps the only city in the world in which one enjoys getting lost.
WILLIAM E. WALLACE
Art historian

Take the walks described by J. G. Links in his superb book, *Venice for Pleasure*.
JOHN JULIUS NORWICH
Historian

4.7 ## Domus
Calle dei Fabbri 4746, ☎041 522 62 59

🎁 Fancy table and kitchen ware. Ground floor is mainly gift-ware, upper floor more serious cooking equipment.
MARCELLA HAZAN
Chef and cookbook author

4.8 ## Palazzo Contarini del Bovolo
Corte dei Risi o del Bovolo
☎041 260 19 74; www.scalabovolo.org
Open April to October.

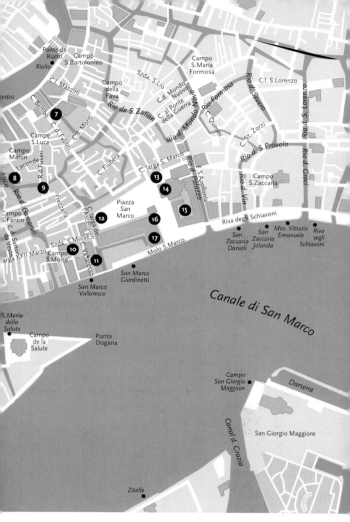

SAN MARCO

1 Corte del Duca Sforza

2 Save Venice Treasure Hunt

3 Rigattieri

4 Museo Fortuny

5 Acqua Pazza

6 Galleria Luce

7 Domus

8 Palazzo Contarini del Bovolo

9 Da Ivo

10 San Moisè

🍽 11 Harry's Bar

12 Museo Correr

🍽 13 The American Bar

14 Basilica di San Marco

15 Doge's Palace (Palazzo Ducale)

16 Museo Archeologico

17 La Biblioteca Marciana (La Zecca)

Staircase
c. 1499, Giovanni Candi

Wandering between Teatro La Fenice and the Campo
Manin you may be lucky enough (helped by some sign-
posts) to come upon the Palazzo Contarini del Bovolo,
which owes its name—*bovolo* means "snail"—to its
fifteenth-century exterior spiral staircase, a unique architectural adornment and a delight to gaze upon, especially
by moonlight, when its marble seems to glow pure white
against the dark wall of the palace.
HELEN F. NORTH
Classicist

Follow the Calle della Vida to the entrance of the Palazzo
Contarini del Bovolo, and go through the alley, Contarini
del Bovolo. Here is an unexpected, astonishing, and beautiful sight—especially on entering from such a dark, narrow
alleyway or *calle*. The elegant circular staircase with arches
above the columns repeats the rhythm of the white stone
arches of the loggia. This open staircase reminds one of the
Tower of Pisa. The architectural elements were reused from
the demolished church of Saint Paternian.
HELEN COSTANTINO FIORATTI
Antiques dealer

4.9 Da Ivo
Ramo dei Fuseri 1809
☎ 041 528 50 04; www.ristorantedaivo.com
Closed Sundays.

🍴🍷 Owner-chef is Tuscan. Best *fiorentina* (firm but very tasty
T-bone steak for two) in town, authoritatively herb-scented
pastas, a sensational mussel soup, charcoal-grilled fish,
fried soft-shell crabs, roast lamb, and, in season, white
truffles and grilled porcini. You might think twice about

ordering the osso bucco, but you are not likely to be disappointed by anything else on the menu.

MARCELLA HAZAN
Chef and cookbook author

Caffè Corretto

🍴 If you're in Venice in the winter and the cold has gone to your bones, one of the cafés will give you your *caffè corretto* with grappa (espresso "corrected" with the addition of grappa).

KEITH CHRISTIANSEN
Chairman of the Department of European Paintings at the Metropolitan Museum of Art

4.10 ## San Moisè
Campo San Moisè
📞 041 528 58 40; www.churchesofvenice.co.uk

Lovers of the Baroque will enjoy the church of San Moisè, with its 1668 façade by Alessandro Tremingnon. Inside are two notable works: Tintoretto's *La Lavanda dei Piedi*, and an altarfront in bronze relief by Niccolò Roccatagliata and his son Sebastiano. Signed and dated 1633, the relief depicts the Deposition.

DAVE KING
Writer

4.11 ## Harry's Bar
Calle Vallaresso 1323
📞 041 528 57 77; www.harrysbarvenezia.com

🍴 It may not produce Venice's most ravishing cooking, but there is no argument about its being the city's most celebrated eatery, the most clubby and glamorous, and the most expensive. Actually, the food can be rather good. If you want to see or be seen you must be seated downstairs

in the bar, where dinner is served after 8 p.m. Some of the
distinguished overflow occasionally ends up on the floor
above. If you make your reservations yourself, ask for the
maître d', Corrado.

MARCELLA HAZAN
Chef and cookbook author

4.12 Museo Correr

Piazza San Marco 52, entrance in Ala Napoleonica
℡ 041 240 52 11; www.museiciviciveneziani.it

Venice is beyond belief—more fantastic than one's most
fanciful inventions. As most of the city is well-known, I
will highly recommend one of its secret places. For reasons
I can't begin to understand, the Museo Correr has been
practically empty when I've gone to Venice, while the
Galleria dell'Accademia has been crowded. The Accademia
is a great museum, true, and it should be seen. But the
Correr is not far behind. It is in the palazzo that defines
one side of the Piazza San Marco, above Florian's, where
elegant people sit by an orchestra, watching the theater of
life. Beyond the Correr's Venetian historical collections, at
the far end and up the stairs again, there is a beautiful
collection with Bellinis and Carpaccios. Carpaccio's
Courtesans is one of the most interesting paintings around,
to my painter's eye. Easel-sized, mysterious, quiet. Felice
Casorati based his 1921 painting *Two Sisters* on this work.

ALAN FELTUS
Painter

4.13 The American Bar

San Marco 302; ℡ 041 522 25 15
Beneath the Torre dell'Orologio

🍴 Humble in appearance, the American Bar has the best
pirini and sandwiches in Venice, which, with a Campari,

makes a perfect morning pit stop. Stand-up and reason-
ably priced, it is streets ahead of its smart neighbors and is
surprisingly little used by foreigners. Kids can ride on the
marble lion.

JOHN CARSWELL
Curator and art historian

4.14 Basilica di San Marco

Piazza San Marco
www.basilicasanmarco.it

The hush of evening falls. The tourists have gone. With
the lights dimmed, the dazzling beauty of the church is
subdued. A few people come in before the evening Mass
and whisper among themselves. Along the wall at the end
of the left transept you sit on a long, plain bench, wood
mounted on stone. Lean against the cool wall. Touch it.
Breathe the silence. Look across the great reach of space
toward the high window, where natural light fades. In the
mysterious half-darkness, the *Madonna Nicopeia* looks
comfortable in her niche, for she has been at home here for
about eight hundred years. Just before the Mass, the lights
go on everywhere, blazing on the mosaics and flooding the
place with a shower of gold. At a very human level, this is
death and rebirth.

MARY JANE PHILLIPS-MATZ
Musicologist and biographer

4.15 Doge's Palace (Palazzo Ducale)

Piazzetta San Marco
☎ 041 271 59 11; www.museiciviciveneziani.it
Secret Itinerary must be reserved in advance.

Pay for a guided tour of the "Secret Itinerary" of the
palace, which takes you to the prison cells, secret passage-
ways, inside the Bridge of Sighs, and, if the group is small

enough, out onto the roof of the palace. There are no railings to speak of, and you can climb the gently sloping lead-sheeted roof for one more spectacular view of San Giorgio. Even without the roof visit, the secret stairways and chambers are a lot of fun.

PABLO CONRAD
Writer and editor

4.16 Museo Archeologico

Piazzetta San Marco 52

☎ 041 522 59 78; www.polomuseale.venezia.beniculturali.it

Enter from the Piazzetta. What's fascinating here is that most of the collection was acquired in the sixteenth century by the Grimani, a Venetian noble family, and bequeathed to the Republic.

RONA GOFFEN
The late Rona Goffen was an art historian.

Marble Gutters

One time, staying in a little *pensione* not far behind San Marco, I looked out the window and was amazed to see that rain gutters along the edges of the rooftops are made of marble. It isn't unbelievable enough that this city was built on stilts in the water, it even has gutters of stone to add weight to its impossible architecture! Venetian Gothic is unlike other Italian Gothic. Canals are unlike other cities' streets. Boats are unlike cars. The resulting effect is magic and quiet elegance: a beauty that makes one smile all the time.

ALAN FELTUS
Painter

4.17 La Biblioteca Marciana (La Zecca)

1547, Jacopo Sansovino
Piazza San Marco 7
☎ 041 240 72 11; www.marciana.venezia.sbn.it

This secret place lies right in the center of the most celebrated piazza in Venice and perhaps the world. To experience a masterpiece of Renaissance architecture by
the renowned Venetian architect Sansovino, request a day
pass as a researcher or student—not a tourist—and leave
a passport at the entry. The former *zecca*, or mint, of the
Venetian Republic houses the national library with its
literary treasure documenting all aspects of Venetian life.
Enjoy sitting under an extensive skylight over the main
reading room and perusing the open stacks. Select a book
at random for an in-depth understanding of an aspect of a
building or a painting perhaps.

MARGARET SPENCER MATZ
Architect

DORSODURO

5.1   San Nicolò dei Mendicoli

Campo San Nicolò

☎ 041 275 03 82

Closed Sundays.

Gloria di San Nicolò

Late 16th century, Francesco Montemezzano

A little-known church in a poor area of the city, San Nicolò dei Mendicoli has a superbly painted ceiling by Francesco Montemezzano, late sixteenth century, with a wooden gilded arcade filled with carved statues.

JOHN JULIUS NORWICH
Historian

5.2   San Raffaele Arcangelo

Campo dell'Arcangelo Raffaele

Storie di Tobiolo

Giovanni Antonio Guardi, c. 1750

The paintings by Guardi on the organ doors of Angelo Raffaele are also well worth a visit.

JOHN JULIUS NORWICH
Historian

5.3   San Sebastiano

Campo San Sebastiano

☎ 041 275 04 62

Closed on Sundays.

Interior painting

Mid- to late-16th century, Paolo Veronese

Veronese's church, decorated with some of his earliest paintings as well as mature works. All beautiful.

RONA GOFFEN
The late Rona Goffen was an art historian.

5.4 Riviera

Fondamenta delle Zattere Ponte Lungo 1473

☏ 041 522 76 21; www.ristoranteriviera.it

🍴 Lovely outdoor location on embankment facing Giudecca canal. Limited outdoor seating. Simple pastas and risottos, good fish, chicken with cardoons sometimes, *fegato alla veneziana* usually.

MARCELLA HAZAN
Chef and cookbook author

5.5 Campo Santa Margherita

Nothing here of great historical interest, no compelling works of art, just an exceptionally spacious and truly popular campo lined with small houses (but some date from the fourteenth century), neighborhood shops, and simple trattorias. Plane trees and benches invite you to enjoy the shade. Closed off at one end by a ruined campanile associated with the church of Santa Margherita, at the other end the Campo leads to a World War I memorial in the form of a flagstaff surrounded by statues of the cardinal virtues.

🍴 The Antico Capon restaurant (east side of the campo) will not disappoint you.

HELEN F. NORTH
Classicist

La Pescheria

Campo Santa Margherita

🍴 No visit to Venice is complete without a visit either to the main fish market (*la Pescheria*) near the Rialto Bridge or to the smaller but in many ways more picturesque one held on the Campo Santa Margherita, near the Carmini. This is a morning activity (they shut up by lunchtime). The Campo Santa Margherita is in a wonderful and lively popular quarter and is very animated.

KEITH CHRISTIANSEN
Chairman of the Department of European Paintings at the Metropolitan Museum of Art

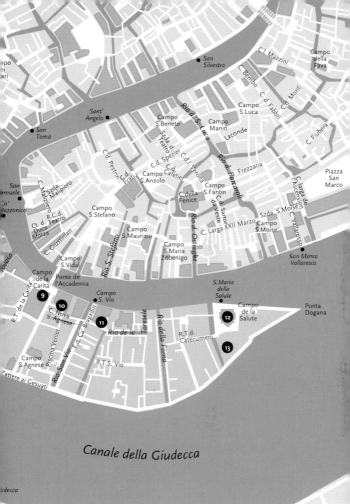

DORSODURO

1. San Nicolò dei Mendicoli
2. San Raffaele Arcangelo
3. San Sebastiano
4. Riviera
5. Campo Santa Margherita
6. Antica Locanda Montin
7. San Trovaso

8. Nico
9. Accademia
10. Trattoria ai Cugnai
11. Galleria Multigraphic
12. Santa Maria della Salute
13. Rio Terrà dei Catecumeni

5.5   Campo Santa Margherita

Pick up any guide to Venice and you are directed straight to the Piazza San Marco. The façade of the Basilica is described in hallowed terms, praise is heaped on the palazzo of the Doges, the campanile, and the clock tower. Every author repeats Napoleon's description of the Piazza as the most elegant drawing room in Europe. Feh! How long since you had a really good time in a drawing room, the eighteenth century? It's the new millennium, and if you want a great experience, turn on your heels and head for the Campo Santa Margherita in the Dorsoduro district.

If the Piazza is the drawing room of Venice, the Campo is the "rec" room. In the evening in San Marco people hold hands to the overture of *The Sound of Music* played by bored musicians at old Florian's café. In Santa Margherita, students and adults crowd together after enjoying club concerts or classical music at the Scuola San Rocco and the Frari. In the Piazza, visitors smile nostalgically at one another while sipping the most expensive cup of coffee in Italy, while in the Campo animated conversation is fueled by fiery grappa or *sgroppino*, an ambrosia produced by whipping lemon sorbet, vodka, and Prosecco (Venetian champagne). In the Piazza, you're next to first-timers and Eurotrash, in the Campo you're arguing with the natives about why the city won't build the moveable barriers to protect their lagoon. San Marco is the fox trot, Santa Margherita is salsa. Don't misunderstand, the Piazza is a beautiful setting with imposing architectural monuments, but when it comes to a good time after the sun sets, there's no place like the Campo. Santa Margherita is a brash, bustling center of activity day and night, a far more accurate measure of Venetian life than the formal presentation of San Marco. One of the most extensive squares in the city, the Campo and its surroundings are a buffet of contemporary culture: everyday activities laced with the vestiges of past glories.

No need to wait for one of those crystalline Venetian days; seek out Santa Margherita on any weekday morning, sunny or overcast, or even in the rain. Enter from the north by crossing the Rio di Cà Foscari, the façade of San Pantalon at your back. You'll encounter a narrow *calle* (lane) lined with shops catering to the everyday needs of the neighborhood, including a *farmacia* and a *latteria* (dairy store) with not only milk and cheeses, but a first-class selection of *vino*, too. Beyond is a lingerie and bathing suit shop (when was the last time anyone willingly entered the water in the lagoon city?) and the Vinaria Nave d'Oro, whose inexpensive table wines are dispensed by siphon from immense glass jugs, but only if you remember to bring an empty! (Okay, occasionally they'll fill up a recycled *acqua minerale* bottle for you, but not without expressing the appropriate Venetian disgust.)

The lane has modern technology, too, including a video automat dispensing tapes to local film junkies day and night. A self-declared no-smoking bar/café serves espresso, cappuccino, wine, and sandwiches while patrons continue to puff away. (In Venice's Marco Polo airport, authorities have placed ashtrays directly beneath the no-smoking signs.) On the truncated tower of the ex-church of Santa Margherita, now part of the university, marble grotesques of a lion and a dragon simultaneously keep ancient demons and truant students at bay.

The vast open space of Santa Margherita spreads to the south, the tiles of the pavement revealing where a canal once crossed the square. Sycamore trees, benches, wellheads, newspaper stands, and food stalls decorate the Campo. A range of human activity is on display—shopping, flirting, children playing and riding bicycles, pensioners relaxing, women kibitzing. Tourists on their way to the Accademia hurry through the square, heedless of its vitality and hidden treasures, and students rush to class, only returning to the Campo in the evening.

Galleries and craft shops co-exist with cafés and groceries. Within the Campo you can view photography, hand-made pottery, and those illusionistic wooden objects—wingtips, ties, jackets—by Loris Marazzi, himself a cottage industry with outlets throughout Venice. More interesting, however, are two troves of Venetian art tucked into the southwest corner of the square. The under-visited fourteenth-century church of Santa Maria dei Carmini (often called, simply, "Chiesa dei Carmine," or "del Carmelo" in the Venetian dialect) contains two marvelous sixteenth-century works. On the left side in the nave is a Lorenzo Lotto altarpiece of *Saint Nicholas and Saints* with a startling bit of landscape below that brings to mind the early panoramic views of Brueghel and Dürer. One of Cima da Conegliano's most compelling paintings is just opposite, the altarpiece of the *Nativity with Saints*, set in a limpid atmosphere that derives from the brilliant landscapes of Giovanni Bellini. A bronze plaque of the Deposition by Francesco di Giorgio Martini, the Sienese Leonardo, is one of the finest of the rare Tuscan works in the city.

Adjacent to the church is the seventeenth-century Scuola Grande dei Carmini, one of the prominent confraternities that provided cradle-to-grave care for Venetians, as well as worthy charities such as orphanages and dowries for the poor. The Scuola contains a striking decorative cycle by Giambattista Tiepolo, the greatest of all late Venetian artists. On the ceiling of the Sala Capitolare, an imperious Virgin bestows the sacred Scapular on the Blessed Simone Stock. Above, Mary is surrounded by a cadre of angels showing a bit much gam, while below, the damned inhabit a Goyesque hell. Who was the Blessed Stock, and what of his scapular vision? According to Carmelite legend, Simon was a thirteenth-century Englishman whose vision of Mary giving him the cloak of the order was accompanied by her promise of salvation to the wearer. The story is inconsequential for us, so sit back and luxuriate in Tiepolo's

grandiose taffeta fantasy, the heavenly drama set in sixteenth-century costume inspired by Veronese. A smaller
ceiling canvas of an angel saving a workman from a fall
depicts an even more obscure story, yet is movingly realized. Displayed in vitrines around the Sala, exceedingly
hideous Murano glass in the shapes of a rooster and eggs
remind us of the mystic marriage of beauty and banality
that surprisingly often informs Italian taste.

However, you're in Santa Margherita for more than
Art with a capital A. Almost anything material or meta-
physical is to be found within this great space. Interested in
something to drink? Try one of the half-dozen cafés that
range from the youthful hangouts of Il Caffè and the
Green Pub to the more stylish banquette and outside seating of the Bar Margaret Duchamp. A quick bite? How
about a slice on the fly at Pizza al Volo, or an outside seat
at one of the two pizzeria/trattorias, watching the ongoing
floor show of the *commedia umana*. Seeking an elegant
dinner? Try L'Incontro, an upper-crust restaurant of
Sardinian descent. Dessert? Rival ice cream emporiums
claim honors for the square, the august Gelateria Caffè
Causin (says right on the awning "founded 1928"), or the
more modern shop on the south side of the Campo with
the air-conditioned back room.

Oh, you prefer to eat in the intimacy of your room?
Of course the contemporary *supermercato* would save you
time, but how pedestrian and unromantic. Better to
patronize the local merchants, the *panificio* (bakery) with
its tortoise-shaped loaves, or the wine shops, or the coffee
and tea vendors, or the curious subterranean stall on the
east side of the Campo that sells only eggs and *acqua
minerale*. Cooking tonight? Try the beef from one of the
butchers, perhaps beneath the beautiful Moorish windows
of the palace at no. 2931. Miró, a sleek black cat, waits
outside the door each morning for his owner to return
from school, hoping for a kindly scratch or scrap of meat.

Prepared *carne*, *pollo*, and *coniglio* (rabbit) also are available from the *macellaio* (butcher) at the southern corner of the Campo.

But as this is the Queen of the Adriatic, fish is a better bet. View the abundance at any of the three fish stalls that occupy the center of Campo Santa Margherita, while gravel-throated fishmongers hawk their seafood to you. Such familiar species as shark, salmon, and shrimp are available, or more exotic delicacies such as *canestri*, *razza*, and *coda di rospo*, the end of the fish. Behind the stalls, on the west wall of the freestanding ex-Scuola of the Varotari (tanner's guild) is a worn stone sign with raised metal letters: LUNGHEZZE MINIME PERMESSE PER LA VENDITA DEL PESCE DELLE SEGUENTI QUALITÀ—the minimum length for the sale of different varieties of fish. Here we find the useful information (in Venetian dialect, of course) that the legal size for *bransin*, *orada*, *dental*, *corbo*, *sparo*, *lovo*, and *boseghetta* is at least five inches long, while *bisatto* must be ten inches, *peocio* only one. The sight of all this piscine flesh make you queasy? No problem, there are several pharmacies available, including the most up-to-date *erborista*, Il Melograno.

Reading matter is as plentiful in the Campo as food, from regular bookshops to the several *edicole* (news stalls) with their dailies and journals and those adult comic books that Italians love. Sundry *cartolerie* sell stationery and art supplies, though the most prominent on the west side of the Campo is more interested in selling Lotto tickets than note paper. A phone shop, two hardware stores, and a lighting shop provide other necessities. On a terrace above the lamp store is the Scuola di Lingua e Cultura Italia, where Venetians learn English, *senza dubbio* so that when you attempt to speak to them in Italian they can demonstrate their Venetian superiority by answering in perfect English. (There is, at times, a faint whiff of the Parisian about the Venetians.) The busy Puntonet, one of the ubiquitous Internet cafés blossoming around town, stands on the east side of the square, just by the art deco façade of the ex-Cinema Moderno. A nearby alley leads to the Corte Del Fontego, with its bricked-up thirteenth-century arches and columns curiously juxtaposed with the local party headquarters of the Rifondazione Comunista.

Exit the Campo by the southeast corner through the Rio Terrà Canal, a designation for streets that were originally canals but have long since been filled. Window-shop past the Mondonovo mask store, but don't be tempted—consider how strange that mask will really look at home. Besides, the masks are an unhappy reminder of the *carnevale* today, that tame excuse intended for the mass tourist trade rather than the gloriously wicked Carnevale of the Republic. Daydream before the ads for weekly apartment and palace rentals at the local realtor. Muse over a pastry from the area's current favorite bakery, the Mantovese Gobbetti, and carry away a characteristic crumb cake or box of biscuits. Peruse the bidets and stylish high-tech *portascopini* (toilet brushes) in a window displaying the latest fashion in bathroom articles. Then mount the steps of the Ponte dei Pugni with its inlaid footprints marking the site of ancient Venetian rites—on this bridge contests were held between rival Venetian factions, the Nicolotti and the Castellani, with each side attempting to push the other over the sides of the unparapeted bridge. Now that would be an annual event worth reviving for tourists. Maybe that bathing suit shop isn't such a bad idea after all.

ERIC DENKER
Art historian

5.6 Antica Locanda Montin

Fondamenta di Borgo 1147
☎ 041 522 71 51; www.locandamontin.com
Closed Tuesday evenings and Wednesdays.

The Antica Locanda Montin, on a quiet canal between Accademia and the station, is a good place to stay—though it tends to be full—and has a very nice restaurant in a vine-covered *cortile* behind (open in summer). The inside spaces are hung with twentieth-century paintings, lesser artists perhaps, but interesting nevertheless. Very pleasant.

ALAN FELTUS
Painter

5.7 San Trovaso

Campo San Trovaso
☎ 041 296 06 30

I particularly like the Tintorettos and the Giambono, *San Giovanni Crisogono*. The Campo di San Trovaso is one of my favorite *campi*, around the corner from the Squero di San Trovaso, one of the few (perhaps by now the only) working gondola boatyards. The walk along the Rio di San Trovaso is lovely, too. The church is one of several Venetian churches with two main entrances, whether to accommodate the idiosyncrasies of the local geography or the rivalries of neighboring groups.

RONA GOFFEN
The late Rona Goffen was an art historian.

5.8 Nico

Zattere ai Gesuati 922; ☎ 041 522 52 93

🍴 To those who like any flavor of ice cream, as long as it's dark chocolate, Venice might claim to be the best *gelato* town in Italy just on the strength of Cipriani's masterpiece. For others, the city doesn't measure up to what you could get in Palermo, Rome, or Bologna. However, it is not quite so poor that you have to give up *gelato* while you are here. There are many stands and *gelaterie* of which the most popular is Nico. Try their chocolate and hazelnut *gianduiotto*.

MARCELLA HAZAN
Chef and cookbook author

5.9   ## Accademia

Campo della Carità

☎ 041 522 22 47; www.polomuseale.venezia.beniculturali.it

Room 20

The Miracle of the True Cross at the Bridge of San Lorenzo

1500, Gentile Bellini

I am partial to Jacopo Bellini's less talented son Gentile. Unlike his kid brother, Giovanni, who can't take his eyes off that strawberry blonde he keeps casting as the Madonna, Gentile makes a polite effort to show the visitor around town, pointing out the sights and performing introductions.

In this painting, he introduces himself (fourth from the left among the gentlemen kneeling out front) and his relatives (or maybe his patrons) and the local celebrities. The portly lady in the left corner—that's Caterina Cornaro, mailed to Cyprus to be its Venetian queen when she was a teenager and yanked back after a widowhood spent under siege from both friend and foe; lined up next to her in strict bosom formation are her ladies in waiting from the toy court at Asolo that Venice gave her as a compensation package for early retirement. The bald chap in the water, managing to stay decorously and effortlessly afloat in contrast to his treading and thrashing companions, is Andrea Vendramin, the Guardian Grande of the Scuola Grande of San Giovanni Evangelista. He has just rescued that confraternity's fragment of the True Cross, which unfortunately fell into the canal while they were parading it around.

Now take a look at the crowd. This is our real introduction to sophisticated Venice. Everybody is standing around marking time. Some are chatting, others are shoving one another on the bridge, and the rest look bored, wondering when the procession is finally going to start up again and how the delay will affect their social plans for the day.

What's the matter with them? Don't they understand

what just happened? Someone dropped a piece of the True Cross into the canal! The True Cross! They took it out for ventilation and veneration, and somebody dropped it off the bridge! Who is responsible? How would you like to be the one who was entrusted to carry the True Cross and let go? What would you say—"I'm sorry?" "Hey, it was an accident?" "It's his fault, he pushed me?" "Look, I said I was sorry, what more do you want?" Now what? How is anybody supposed to find a piece of old wood if it sinks into all that junk that accumulates at the bottom of a canal?

Never mind—no use getting all worked up. These things happen. They found it, thanks to a miracle; the parade got going again, and people made it to their lunch dates.

The Scuola still has its relic of the True Cross. The porter told me he would have to go get the key and there really wasn't that much to look at and it was getting on to lunchtime—but he would go if I insisted.

JUDITH MARTIN
Journalist

5.10   Trattoria ai Cugnai
Calle Nova Sant'Agnese; ☎ 041 528 92 38
Closed Mondays.

🍴 In Venetian, the word *cugnai* means "brothers-in-law" and "sisters-in-law." Here you have both, in a plain, honest Venetian family that has run this restaurant for decades. My son and daughters were children when we first moved to Venice and began sitting at the big, family-sized tables; now they are past thirty. The *cugnai* hand you a simple menu of food that they cook in their tiny kitchen. No new cuisine; no newfangled anything; just the same blessed Venetian fare, year after year.

MARY JANE PHILLIPS-MATZ
Musicologist and biographer

An 18th-Century Itinerary

Start with the Ca' Rezzonico, the stupendous palace on the Grand Canal designed by Longhena in the seventeenth century, but completely decorated in the eighteenth and today the museum of the eighteenth century. There are spectacular ceilings by Tiepolo, fantastical furniture by the brilliant Brustolon, and dazzling rooms. Then head to the Scuola dei Carmini for one of the most suggestive ambiences in the city. The scuole were typically Venetian lay confraternities. Perhaps the most visited one is the Scuola di San Giorgio degli Schiavoni, with its wonderful series of canvases by Carpaccio. The Scuola dei Carmini is more intact and carries you into the eighteenth century. The ceiling of the second floor is decorated with dazzling canvases by Tiepolo. The furniture and furnishings are intact. Opposite the entrance to the Scuola is a good place to buy your supply of grappa before you head to the church of the Gesuati on the Zattere—beautiful in the late afternoon light. For those who think art stopped in Venice in the sixteenth century, this church serves as a warning. The work of the great neo-Palladian architect Giorgio Massari, it is grand, airy, spacious, and scenographic, and in every way a worthy successor to Palladio's churches of San Giorgio Maggiore and the Redentore—the latter clearly visible from its front steps.

The Gesuati has a wonderful light in the morning and afternoon. The ceiling is divided into compartments with spectacular frescoes by Tiepolo (center scene shows Saint Dominic instituting the Rosary while the Madonna and her healthy child look on from the clouds; the smaller picture fields the Apotheosis of Saint Dominic and Saint Dominic Praying to the Virgin). On the first altar on the right is one of Tiepolo's religious masterpieces: the *Madonna and Child with Saints* (1748). It reaches all the way back to Bellini for the architectural setting of the figures, which is fifteenth-century and plays against Massari's eighteenth-century

architecture. The third altar on the right has a splendid altarpiece by Piazzetta—who played Caravaggio to Tiepolo's Carracci. The church also contains an almost unique opportunity to see what Venetian sculptors were doing in the eighteenth century. The statues in the niches and the reliefs with biblical stories are by Morlaiter—a contemporary of Tiepolo's and wonderfully gifted. In short, this church encapsulates eighteenth-century Venetian art in a way equaled only by Massari's other great ecclesiastical masterpiece, the oval-shaped church of the Pietà, which you may wish to dash over to see after having your eyes opened here (concerts are given in the Pietà, and this may be something to keep in mind, especially since Vivaldi was associated with the church, which had a famous school of female musicians and singers who performed from behind the grilled balconies). Like Ruskin, I love Byzantine Venice, medieval Venice, and Renaissance Venice, but unlike Ruskin, I would be hard-pressed to think Baroque and eighteenth-century Venice any less enthralling.
KEITH CHRISTIANSEN
Chairman of the Department of European Paintings at the Metropolitan Museum of Art

ITINERARY:
1. Ca' Rezzonico Fondamenta, Rezzonico
2. Scuola Grande dei Carmini, Campo Carmini
3. Gesuati Fondamenta delle Zattere
4. La Pietà Riva degli Sciavone

5.11 Galleria Multigraphic

728 de la Chiesa San Vio; ☎ 041 528 51 59

A few minutes' stroll from the Peggy Guggenheim Collection at the Palazzo Venier Dei Leoni, in the direction of the Accademia Bridge, is the unpretentious but very special Galleria Multigraphic. There is a nineteenth-century printing press in one room. Owned by Luciano de March, the gallery exhibits both original works and graphics by contemporary Italian and European artists. Among them are Mario Palli, whose abstract works are striking, and Giuseppe Santomaso, a native Venetian who died in 1990 and was a friend of Peggy's. There is a photo of him in the Guggenheim café. He was honored by Venice with an exhibition at the Museo Correr in 1982.

Art is a constant, vital force in the everyday life of Venetians. Before returning to your hotel, take a moment for a prayer of gratitude at Santa Maria della Salute for all this beauty—past and present.

NICHOLAS ARCOMANO
Attorney

5.12   Santa Maria della Salute

1631–1687, Baldassare Longhena
Campo della Salute
☏ 041 274 39 28; www.sacred-destinations.com

Eighteenth-century Venice is about sophisticated theatrical artifice. It's also about lightness and delicacy and intrigue. Baldassare Longhena's masterpiece, the perfect monument to mark the beginning of the incomparable promenade that is the Grand Canal, was completed in 1687 (five years after his death), and no single monument is more responsible for ushering in that golden period of the eighteenth century than this one.

The church was actually commissioned to commemorate the city's deliverance from the brutal plague of 1630. Longhena wrote that he designed the building with a circular plan in order to symbolize a crown dedicated to the Blessed Virgin. The building is always glorious and sets the tone of your visit to Venice in any season, but it is really at its best on November 21 (the *festa della Salute*), when the main doors are wide open and the interior brightly lit in the evening light, and seaworthy Venetians hobble across the canal upon a temporary fabric-draped walkway atop a makeshift chain of boats to visit the church.

That kind of Venetian *scenografia* is nearly enough to make you forget that this elegant setting did not come about as naturally and easily as it may seem. The Venetians worked hard to achieve this lightness. Documents attest to the fact that no fewer than 1,156,627 tree trunks from the Dolomites were driven into the muck and cut off flush to create a platform on which to build the church and the entrance plaza.

Dazzling though all this may be, there is more: namely, three altarpieces by Luca Giordano (to the right as you enter) and a *Pentecost* by Titian (on the left as you enter). The Titian comes from the suppressed church of Santo Spirito in Isola, as do the others on the ceiling of the Sacristy. These date from the 1540s while the altarpiece (on panel) is one of Titian's earliest, dating from c. 1510. The Sacristy also contains Tintoretto's fine *Marriage at Cana* and two wonderfully fresh *bozzetti* by Luca Giordano for his altarpieces in the church. A small twelfth-century Byzantine icon that originally hung in the Hagia Sophia in Constantinople has been removed recently for restoration.

GEORGE BISACCA
Conservator of paintings

5.13 Rio Terrà dei Catecumeni
Near the bridge of Santa Maria della Salute

The living room of the San Gregorio neighborhood, this spacious square faces the Giudecca Canal. For most of the day, you sit quietly, away from noise and clutter. Partly shaded, partly sunny, Catecumeni offers peace as waves from the *zattere* break over the *fondamenta*. Then several women gather, and suddenly there is pandemonium as noisy children tumble out of the elementary school run by nuns of the Le Salesie di Padova order. Out come book bags, jump ropes, and balls; dogs bark. Then gradually everyone drifts away toward the Salute or into the Calle dell'Abbazia or Calle dei Spezieri, and peace returns.

MARY JANE PHILLIPS-MATZ
Musicologist and biographer

Echo

It's not that you're encircled by water; it's more that everything is swirling, like Tintoretto in his quest to capture everything at one time in defiance of space and time.

Perspective? Venice is the place. Street names resist. Palaces and piazzas collapse into one another. The harbor shape-shifts in the mist. Nowhere is it easier to get lost. My attention is enticed, incited, to circle, to keep roving, if not like the water itself around the fixed points of the quays, then like the palaces on the Grand Canal, the gondolas, taxis, vaporetto, police boats, wherries top-heavy with mounds of cement and crisscrossed planks, and other water-bound vehicles, that swirl like brushstrokes in action across the canals and wider reaches of the Adriatic.

Siena, an homage to stasis; Venice, an homage to kinesis. That is why Tintoretto and Turner and Carpaccio are its truest masters and not the—however brilliant and accurate—Canaletto and Gaudi. Swollen with the remnants of ancient enthusiasms, Venice offers distraction that is not without soul. Everything that happens in Venice happens more than once. This doubling forces you to notice the slight changes that occur moment to moment, and enforces this with noises that, thanks to the acoustic richness of the place, could originate out on the water or in a bar, like this clatter of plates, the clank of spoon against cup in the (perfectly Italian) "India Cafe."

MARK RUDMAN
Poet, essayist, and translator

VENETIAN ISLANDS

GIUDECCA

6.1 ## Church of the Redentore
1577–1592, Andrea Palladio

The church of the Redentore, by Palladio (completed after his death), was built in gratitude for salvation from the Plague and is best visited the third Sunday in July, during the Feast of the Redeemer. You should do it right, starting on the San Marco side of the canal, and crossing the pontoon bridges built for the occasion to take you over the Grand Canal and the Giudecca Canal to the church. If you do this, you will probably not get the Plague (it's worked for me).

RONA GOFFEN
The late Rona Goffen was an art historian.

Watching the Ships Go By

For my money, watching the ships go by is the best thing to be done in Venice, and it is best done by sitting on the quayside below the Dogana, at the tip of the Giudecca. From here you can see in your mind's eye the gilded galleons of *la Serenissima* returning from the east, trailing the ensigns of defeated enemies, and in your real eye the great, gaudy cruise ships that, sailing in hardly less splendidly, bring yet more wondering pilgrims to this seaport of delight.

JAN MORRIS
Historian and writer

6.2 ### Hotel Cipriani
Giudecca 10
☎ 041 520 77 44; www.hotelcipriani.com

🍴♙ It is the place to go for the best chocolate ice cream in
the world; see the recipe in *Marcella's Italian Kitchen*. The
hotel's new casual restaurant/pizzeria is called Cip's. The
tables on the embankment face Venice and offer what may
be the most breathtaking view ever to come with pizza.
This is the place to try the best grappas made.
MARCELLA HAZAN
Chef and cookbook author

Swimming Pools
Piscina Comunale Sant'Alvise, in the Centro Sportivo,
Carnnaregio 3163
☎ 041 71 56 50; www.ilcentrosantalvise.com
Piscina Amedeo Chimisso, Centro Sportivo Sacca San Biagio
☎ 041 528 54 30; www.comune.venezia.it
In Italian pools, swimmers must wear caps; flip-flops or
plastic sandals are required in the shower room.

Being a passionate swimmer, I often travel with swimsuit
and goggles. Perhaps others would be interested in Venice's
two, modern, clean twenty-five-meter public pools. They
both have regularly-scheduled forty-five- to ninty-minute
minute periods of free swim (in addition to classes). Single
swims cost seventy-five-hundred lire; a larger investment
of sixty-five- to seventy-thousand lire buys a ten-swim
ticket good for three months. One is in Cannaregio, at
Sant'Alvise, and the other is on the Giudecca at Sacca
Fisola, Campo San Gerardo. Both are easily reached by
vaporetto, and the latter has a beautiful view of the
lagoon; one whole wall is glass.
SALLY SPECTOR
Artist

ITALY

TORCELLO

BURANO

MURANO

SAN ERASMO

SAN
MICHELE

VENEZIA

Porto di Lido

LIDO

LA GIUDECCA

F.S.Biaggio   S. Eufemia

F.S.Eufemia

Giudecca

Canale della Giudecca

F.S.Eufemia

Redentore

Campo
S.Cosmo

F. San Giacomo

Campo
del S.S.
Redentore

Corti
Grandi

Rio Pallada

1

Rio d. S.Eufemia

Rio d. Ponte Piccolo

Rio d. Ponte Lungo

LA GIUDECCA

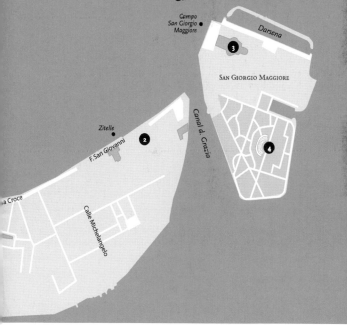

Canale Di San Marco

Campo San Giorgio Maggiore

Darsena

San Giorgio Maggiore

Zitelle

Canal d. Grazia

F.San Giovanni

Calle Michelangelo

a Croce

VENETIAN ISLANDS

GIUDECCA
1   Church of the Redentore
2   Hotel Cipriani

SAN GIORGIO MAGGIORE
3   San Giorgio Maggiore
4   Teatro Verde

SAN GIORGIO MAGGIORE

`6.3` San Giorgio Maggiore
Begun 1565, Andrea Palladio
☎ 041 522 78 27

Maybe Palladio's greatest church and one of the master-pieces of Renaissance architecture; while you're waiting for the vaporetto to go back to Venice, you get a great view of the city.

RONA GOFFEN
The late Rona Goffen was an art historian.

`6.4` Teatro Verde
Isola di San Giorgio Maggiore

A unique and scenic Teatro di Verzura (Theater on the Green) to be enjoyed during summer Biennale dance and music seasons.

GIANFRANCO MOSSETTO
Merchant banker

SAN MICHELE (ISLAND OF THE DEAD)

Grave of Joseph Brodsky
Cemetery of San Michele

Visit the grave of Joseph Brodsky (1940–1996) in the section set aside for foreigners in the Cemetery of San Michele on the Island of the Dead. The 1987 Nobel Laureate in Literature, regarded by many as the greatest Russian poet of his generation, was as well a great English essayist and American citizen, and was buried here according to his own wish. Read *Watermark* (1992), which he wrote in and about Venice.

ADELE CHATFIELD-TAYLOR
President of the American Academy in Rome

TORCELLO

From far across the lagoon, the church of Torcello rises, linking the great horizontal expanses of low-lying marshes and lowering sky. The scene reminds us of the earliest history of Venice when a tiny, local population took refuge in the safety of the remote islands. There they built one of the gems of Romanesque Europe: the church and baptistery of Torcello with its spectacular mosaics.

WILLIAM E. WALLACE
Art historian

Santa Maria dell'Assunta
Piazza di Torcello
West wall
www.sacred-destinations.com

Last Judgment Mosaics (Giudizio Universale)
12th century

Venice is so choked with tourists that it is a relief to wander a bit farther afield. The mosaic of the *Final Judgment* in the Basilica on the island of Torcello merits a half day to itself. Of particular interest in this Byzantine epoch mosaic is the depiction of the dead souls being tormented in hell—visibly the clergy, the rich, and Turkish-looking infidel types. See how the infernal fires well up from Christ's throne and snake their way through the mosaic's panels to the scenes of torment. This Last Judgment is a worthy contrast to Michelangelo's version in every respect.

GREGORY S. BUCHER
Classicist

Excursion to the Venetian Lagoon

A visit to the islands in the lagoon—by vaporetto, motorboat, or *sandalo* (rowboat)—should be the crown of any Venetian sojourn, but so rich is this trip that precious

details may be overlooked. Here are a few from the islands
in the distant northern part of the lagoon.

When you disembark at Burano, Browning's matchless
assessment of the Venetians in "A Toccata of Galuppi's"
may be lurking in your memory:

> As for Venice and her people, merely
>   born to bloom and drop,
> Here on earth they bore their fruitage,
>   mirth and folly were the crop:
> What of soul was left, I wonder, when
>   the kissing had to stop?

Look for the half-length statue of Galuppi himself,
Il Buranello, or "the little fellow from Burano," setup
only recently in the piazza close to the landing stage. Then
go into the church of San Martino on your left, seek out
the oratory of Santa Barbara in the north aisle, and gaze
at the young Giambattista Tiepolo's huge *Crucifixion*, a
miracle of dramatic composition and somber color. Note
the oval frame in the lower left with a portrait of the
donor, who looks at you but points to the painting he has
commissioned. Then walk a few hundred yards down the
spacious via Baldassare Galuppi to the restaurant Da
Romano and sample the freshest fish in the world, quite
possibly presented for your choice swimming in a washtub.

A five-minute ride by vaporetto takes you to Torcello,
where—between the departure of one vaporetto and the
arrival of the next—you may have the island not to
yourself, but relatively uncrowded. Among the glories of
Torcello is Santa Maria Assunta, the cathedral founded in
639 when the future Venetians fled from Altinum on the
mainland before the Lombard invaders. Once you have
studied the twelfth-century mosaics representing the
Universal Judgment on the west wall and the Byzantine
Madonna on her golden ground in the central apse behind

the altar, look closely at the pulpit and the fragments that support it. These are perhaps from the earliest church on this site, perhaps even from the mainland. At the base of the pulpit stair note the relief (clumsily reconstructed) representing Occasio (the Greek Kairos). His feet are planted on winged wheels, one hand holds a set of balances, and the man standing in front of him grasps his forelock. But two figures behind him (a man and a woman) have missed their chance, and the woman turns away in tears. Another fragmentary relief (on the choir enclosure) shows a figure turning on a wheel—Ixion, so rarely depicted even on Greek vases that he is seldom recognized here. Outside once more, seat yourself for a moment on the throne of Attila (thus guaranteeing your return to Torcello) and then enjoy, not just the food and drink provided by the Locanda Cipriani nearby, but the view across their garden to Santa Fosca with its octagonal portico.

If you search for genuine solitude in the lagoon today, best to seek out the well-named island of San Francesco del Deserto, a twenty-minute ride by *sandalo* from Burano, where an active community of Franciscans serves a church associated with a visit by Saint Francis of Assisi on his way back from the Orient. A pine tree is said to have grown from the staff he planted in the ground. Cypress trees, well-tended flower borders, and benches close to the shore invite the visitor to rest and ponder the island's felicitous motto: *O beata solitudo, O sola beatitudo!*

HELEN F. NORTH
Classicist

ITINERARY:
1. Venice to Burano, take no. 12 from Fondamente Nuove or no. 4 from San Zaccaria
2. Burano to Torcello, take no. 14
3. Burano to San Francesco del Deserto, take the local boat

SAN LAZZARO DEGLI ARMENI

Monastery
Open 3 p.m. to 5 p.m. daily.

Home of Mechitarists (the Armenian Catholics), San Lazzaro has the third-largest Armenian manuscript library in the world, a marvelous collection of Kütahya eighteenth-century pottery, and a charming garden. Byron used to row across the lagoon and helped the monks produce the first Armenian/English dictionary. You can take the vaporetto from Venice or hire a rowboat from the Lido.

JOHN CARSWELL
Curator and art historian

INDEX OF CONTRIBUTORS

The late BETH VAN HOESEN ADAMS was a prominent artist and print-maker. She was the recipient of the City of San Francisco Award of Honor in Graphics and the California Society of Printmakers Distinguished Arts Award. p. 44

ROSS ANDERSON is the founder of the award-winning design firm Anderson Architects. He is the recipient of numerous awards, including the Rome Prize in Architecture from the American Academy in Rome. He has taught at Yale, Columbia, and Carnegie Mellon universities, and at the Parsons School of Design. p. 31

NICHOLAS ARCOMANO is a former Senior Attorney at BMI, vice president and counsel at SESAC, Inc., specializing in copyright law, and former contributing editor to *Dance Magazine*. pp. 94, 118

LIDIA MATTICCHIO BASTIANICH is one of the mostloved chefs on television, a best-selling cookbook author, and restaurateur. She has held true to her Italian roots and culture, which she proudly and warmly invites others to experience. Her cookbooks include *Lidia's Italy* and *Lidia's Italian Table*. pp. 22, 34

JACK BEAL is an American realist painter whose works are found in public collections throughout the U.S., including the Metropolitan Museum of Art, the Museum of Modern Art, and the Whitney Museum of American Art. p. 62

GEORGE BISACCA is a conservator of paintings at the Metropolitan Museum of Art in New York. pp. 10, 119

KATEY BROWN is the director of the Johnston-Felton-Hay House in Macon, Georgia. She is a former curator of the Historic Macon Foundation and taught art history on University of Georgia's Study Abroad Program in Cortona, Italy. p. 14

GREGORY S. BUCHER is a classicist. He is a Fellow of the American Academy in Rome, the Center for Hellenic Studies, and the American School of Classical Studies, Athens. p. 127

MICHAEL CADWELL is professor of architecture at the Knowlton School of Architecture, The Ohio State University. p. 58

JOHN CARSWELL, retired director of the Islamic Department at Sotheby's London, was professor of fine arts at the American University of Beirut for twenty years, curator of the Oriental Institute, and director of the David and Alfred Smart Museum at the University of Chicago. He is a professor of the history of art and archaeology at the University of London. pp. 100, 130

ADELE CHATFIELD-TAYLOR is a historic preservationist, writer, and the president of the American Academy in Rome. pp. 40, 126

KEITH CHRISTIANSEN is chairman of the Department of European

Paintings at the Metropolitan Museum of Art, where, over the course of more than three decades, he has organized numerous exhibitions and written widely on Italian painting. He has taught at Columbia University and the Institute of Fine Arts of New York University. pp. 69, 70, 99, 105, 117

PABLO CONRAD is a teacher and writer living in New York City. p. 101

FRANCESCA DELL'ACQUA is a professor of medieval art at the Università de Salerno. She is a Fellow of the American Academy in Rome. pp. 19, 53

ERIC DENKER is the curator of prints and drawings at the Corcoran Gallery of Art in Washington, D.C. He is a professor in the Corcoran College of Art and Design's Summer Study Abroad Program in Italy, a senior lecturer in the Education Division at the National Gallery of Art, treasurer of the Print Council of America, and an adjunct professor in the Liberal Studies Program at Georgetown University. pp. 85, 108

JUDITH DiMAIO is dean of the School of Architecture and Design at the New York Institute of Technology. pp. 17, 24

MARY ANN HAICK DiNAPOLI is a historian and genealogist. She recently served on the project team for the Museum of the City of New York's exhibit, "A Community of Many Worlds: Arab Americans in New York City." She is a cofounder of the Friends of the Lower West Side, a group that seeks to preserve the rich immigrant history of downtown Manhattan's Lower West Side, the first center of Arab immigration to the United States. pp. 15, 76

KATHE DYSON and her husband own and operate the Williams Selyem Winery in Sonoma County, California, as well as Villa Pillo, a small winery in Tuscany. pp. 22, 49

GERALDINE ERMAN is an sculptor. She is a recipient of a Guggenehim Fellowship and a Rome Prize form the American Academy in Rome. p. 27

RICHARD L. FEIGEN is an art collector and dealer. His gallery, Richard L. Feigen & Company, is based in New York City. For more than fifty years, he has been collecting and dealing a wide range of work—from Old Master drawings to contemporary works. He is the author of the acclaimed memoir *Tales from the Art Crypt: The Painters, the Museums, the Curators, the Collectors, the Auctions, the Art.* pp. 31, 49

ALAN FELTUS taught at the American University in Washington, D.C., from 1972 to 1984. A recipient of the Rome Prize for Painting from the American Academy in Rome in 1970, he moved to Italy permanently in 1987. He has been represented by Forum Gallery in New York since the mid-seventies. pp. 100, 102, 113

HELEN COSTANTINO FIORATTI founded L'Antiquaire in 1965, which then merged with the Connoisseur in 1982. The gallery deals in all varieties of decorative arts and antiques from Byzantine mosaics to Italian and French eighteenth-century furniture and Old Master drawings. She is the co-author of *French Antiques* and *The History of Italian Furniture*, and frequently lectures on decorative arts at museums across the country. pp. 23, 30, 31, 42, 44, 49, 50, 52, 53

The late RONA GOFFEN was among the most distinguished art historians of the Italian Renaissance. She was the Board of Governors Professor of Art History at Rutgers University, served on the executive board of the Renaissance Society of America, and was a member of the board of advisers of the Center for Advanced Study in the Visual Arts at the National Gallery of Art. Her books include *Piety and Patronage in Renaissance Venice* and *Renaissance Rivals*. Her many honors include fellowships from the American Academy in Rome, the National Endowment for the Humanities, and the Guggenheim Foundation. pp. 15, 22, 31, 32, 42, 59, 63, 64, 69, 75, 79, 83, 84, 88, 90, 93, 102, 104, 114, 122, 126

ALEXANDER GORLIN is principal and founder of Alexander Gorlin Architects in New York City. The firm has won numerous awards, most notably AIA Design Awards for the House in the Rocky Mountains, Ruskin Place town house, North Shore Hebrew

Academy, and the Southampton House. p. 36

BEATRICE H. GUTHRIE has been on the board of directors of Save Venice for thirteen years. She is Cavaliere of the Italian Republic. pp. 77, 90, 92

MARCELLA HAZAN has received lifetime achievement awards from the James Beard Foundation and the International Association of Culinary Professionals (IACP), as well as a knighthood from her own country. She is the author of six classic cookbooks and conducted her own cooking school for nearly thirty years. pp. 66, 68, 69, 74, 75, 76, 77, 78, 84, 93, 94, 95, 98, 99, 105, 114, 123

EMILIE K. JOHNSON is currently a Ph.D. candidate in art and architectural history at the University of Virginia. Previously, she worked at several art museums including the Corcoran Gallery of Art in Washington, D.C., and the Williams College Museum of Art in Williamstown, Massachusetts. pp. 79, 83

DAVE KING is the author of *The Ha-Ha*, named one of the best books of 2005 by *The Christian Science Monitor*, *The Washington Post*, the *Pittsburgh Tribune-Review*, and other publications. He is recipient of the John Guare Writer's Fund Rome Prize Fellowship from the American Academy of Arts and Letters. p. 99

SUSAN KLEINBERG is an artist based in New York City whose work has been shown internationally. She is a

Fellow of the American Academy in Rome. pp. 16, 37, 68, 74, 83

SWIETLAN NICHOLAS KRACZYNA is an artist and printmaker. His art is deeply rooted in the traditions of the Italian Renaissance. He is one of the founders of Il Bisonte International School of Advanced Printmaking in Florence, Italy, where he lives. pp. 21, 52

Painter JOHN LEAVEY's many honors include a Lewis Comfort Tiffany Grant and a Fellowship from the American Academy in Rome. His work has been exhibited extensively in both the U.S. and Italy, and can be found in the permanent collections of, among others, the Hirshhorn Collection in Washington, D.C., and the Museo della Citta da Roma. p. 21

ROBERT LIVESEY is an architect and a professor at the Knowlton School of Architecture at Ohio State University. p. 35

BARBARA LYNN-DAVIS is an art historian and writer. Her many honors include a Certificate for Distinction in Teaching from the Faculty of Arts and Sciences at Harvard University. The selections included in this book are drawn from her manuscript, *Illuminations: A Travelers Guide to the Art of Italy*. p. 88

THOMAS F. MADDEN is a professor of medieval history and the director of the Center for Medieval and Renaissance Studies at Saint Louis University. His many honors include a National Endowment for the Humanities Grant and the Gladys

Krieble Delmas Foundation Grant for Research in Venice and the Veneto. p. 63

JUDITH MARTIN writes the Miss Manners column on etiquette, which is distributed three times a week by United Features Syndicate and carried in more than two hundred newspapers worldwide. Before she began the advice column, she was a journalist, covering social events at the White House; she then became a theater and film critic. In 2006, she was a special guest correspondent on The Colbert Report, giving her analysis of the manners with which the White House Press Corps spoke to the president. p. 115

MARGARET SPENCER MATZ is an architect, and visiting professor of architecture at Pratt Institute. pp. 85, 103

D. B. MIDDLETON is a design principal and partner at Handel Architects. He has taught and lectured at numerous universities, including Harvard, Yale, Syracuse, and the University of Virginia. He is the recipient of the Rome Prize from the American Academy in Rome. p. 54

JAN MORRIS is an historian, travel writer, and the author of forty books, including *Venice*, a cultural history of Venice. p. 122

GIANFRANCO MOSSETTO is a scholar and a merchant banker with extensive experience in real estate. He has served as Chancellor for the Arts of the City of Venice, and taught Public Finance and Art Economics at Cà Foscari University for many years. pp. 74, 126

HELEN F. NORTH is professor emerita of classics at Swarthmore College. pp. 91, 98, 105, 127

JOHN JULIUS NORWICH's many books include *The Normans in Sicily*; *A History of Venice*; and a three-volume history of the Byzantine Empire. He has written and presented some thirty historical documentaries for television, and is a regular lecturer on Venice. He is chairman of the Venice in Peril Fund, co-chairman of the World Monuments Fund, and a Commendatore of the Ordine al Merito della Repubblica Italiana. He was made a CVO in 1993. pp. 90, 95, 104

JANE OLIENSIS is the founder and director of Humanities Spring, an interdisciplinary travel-study summer program in Assisi, Italy, and New York City. She has published poems and translations both in Italy and the U.S. She teaches at the Università di Perugia, in the Facoltà di Scienze Linguistiche, and lives in the hills outside Assisi with her family. p. 43

JACQUELINE OSHEROW is the author of several collections of poetry, including *Hoopoe's Crown* and *Looking for Angels in New York*. She was awarded the Witter Bynner Prize by the American Academy and Institute of Arts and Letters and fellowships from the Guggenheim Foundation, the National Endowment for the Arts, and the Ingram Merrill Foundation. pp. 28, 38, 43, 70, 74

PAUL PASCAL is professor emeritus of classics at the University of Washington, where he specialized in medieval Latin studies. He is a Fellow of the American Academy in Rome. p. 93

MARY JANE PHILLIPS-MATZ, musicologist and biographer, is the author of *Puccini A Biography*, *Rosa Ponselle: American Diva*, and *Verdi A Biography*, which won the Royal Philharmonic Prize. She is the co-founder of the American Institute for Verdi Studies at New York University and consultant and lecturer to the Metropolitan Opera, the Washington National Opera, and the San Francisco Opera, among others. She has contributed to *Opera News* for over fifty years. pp. 101, 116, 120

DANA PRESCOTT is a painter, writer, and educator. She was director of Rhode Island School of Design's European Honors Program for many years and served as Andrew Heiskell Arts Director at the American Academy in Rome for five years. She has taught on the Rome faculty of Cornell University and Temple University, among others. She is executive director of the Civitella Ranieri Foundation in Umbria. pp. 21, 39, 47

GILLIAN PRICE is the author of three guides on the Italian Alps, one on Tuscany, and another on Sicily. p. 76

The principal historian for the Emmy-nominated PBS series *Renaissance*, THEODORE K. RABB is emeritus professor at Princeton University. pp. 30, 87

LESLIE RAINER is a wall-paintings conservator. She received an M.A. in the Conservation of Decorated Architectural Surfaces, and certificates in Mural Paintings Conservation from ICCROM, and has worked on projects worldwide. She is a Fellow of the American Academy in Rome. pp. 26, 28

MARK RUDMAN's books of poetry include *Quintet: Sundays on the Phone*, *The Couple*, *Provoked in Venice*, *Millennium Hotel*, and *Rider*, which won the National Book Critics Circle Award. He is editor in chief of *Pequod*, an international literary journal, and the recipient of awards from the Ingram Merrill Foundation, Guggenheim Foundation, and National Endowment for the Arts. He teaches poetry at New York University. p. 121

SALLY SPECTOR has taught art history and drawing to several study-abroad programs in Italy. She is an artist and the author of *Venice and Food*, and *Chocolate, Truffles, and Other Treasures of Italy's Piedmont Cuisine*. pp. 65, 123

SALLIE TISDALE is the author of, among other books, *The Best Thing I Ever Tasted: The Secret of Food* and *Women of the Way: Discovering 2,500 Years of Buddhist Wisdom*. Her work frequently appears in such periodicals

as *Condé Nast Traveler*, *New York Times Magazine*, and *The Antioch Review*. She is a contributing editor of *Harper's* as well as a columnist for the online magazine *Salon*. She has received numerous awards and honors, including a fellowship from the National Endowment for the Arts. p. 27

WILLIAM E. WALLACE is the Barbara Murphy Bryant Distinguished Professor of Art History at Washington University in St. Louis. He has published extensively on Renaissance art and is an internationally recognized authority on Michelangelo. pp. 32, 35, 48, 63, 95, 127

FRED WESSEL is a professor of art at the Hartford Art School at the University of Hartford. He co-directs workshops in Italy, bringing small groups of artists and artlovers to Tuscany and Umbria. His work is included in many private and public collections including the Museum of Modern Art, the Brooklyn Museum, and the Philadelphia Museum of Art. pp. 20, 22, 37

ANN THOMAS WILKINS has taught in the Department of Classics at Duquesne University in Pittsburgh and on Duquesne's Rome campus for many years. Her interests span from ancient Greece and Rome to Mussolini's Italy and nineteenth- and twentieth-century American architecture. pp. 16, 41, 42

DAVID G. WILKINS is professor emeritus of the history of art and architecture at the University of

Pittsburgh; recently he has taught on Duquesne University's campus in Rome. He has taught and led tours to Rome, Florence, and other destinations for many years. pp. 16, 42

JOHN L. WONG is managing principal and chairman of the board of the award-winning firm SWA Group, Landscape Architecture, Planning, and Urban Design. He has taught at Harvard University and the University of California, Berkeley. pp. 26, 36, 47, 50, 78

SUSAN WOOD is a professor of art history at Oakland University in Michigan. She is a Fellow of the American Academy of Rome, and travels to Italy frequently for her research on Roman sculpture. pp. 41, 45

INDEX

FLORENCE

Acciaioli, Niccolo 51
Annunciation (Pontormo) 20
Arcetri 49
Arciconfraternita della Misericordia 15
Baldovinetti, Alesso 46
Bardi Chapel Frescoes (Giotto) 43
Benedetto da Maiano 44
Biblioteca Mediceo-Laurenziana 35
Boboli Garden (Giardino di Boboli) 18, 26, 39
Brunelleschi 10, 20, 34, 42, 44
Buontalenti 26
Campo di Marte 49
Cappella Brancacci 28
Cappella Capponi 20
Cappella Sassetti 33
Cappelle Medicee 36
Carmignano 49
Cenacoli (Last Suppers) 32
La Certosa del Galluzzo 51
Chapel of the Cardinal of Portugal 46
City Center East 42
City Center North 34
City Center West 30
Cione, Nardo di 31
Colli 45
Corridoio Vasariano 17
del Tasso, Marco 26
della Robbia, Luca 38, 46, 53
Deposition (Pontormo) 20
Dome, Santa Maria del Fiore 10
Duomo 10
Fiesole 50
Flood Marker 42
Fondazione Horne 42
Fortini, Davide 26
Frescoes, Bardi Chapel 43
Galluzzo 51
Galleria degli Uffizi 17
Ghirlandaio, Domenico 30, 33

Giotto 42, 43
Gozzoli, Benozzo 38
Grotta Grande del Buontalenti 26
Grotticina di Madama 26
Historic Center 10
Hotels
    Hotel Lungarno 24
    Hotel Orto de' Medici 39
    Pensione Sorelle Bandini 28
Il Corridoio Vasariano 17
Impruneta 52
Lapi, Zanobi 47, 54
Last Judgement (Nardo di Cione) 31
Last Supper (Ghirlandaio) 30
Maiano, Benedetto da 44
Masaccio 28, 31
Medici Villas 47
Michelangelo 35, 37
Mercato Centrale 34
Michelozzo 12, 38, 47, 50
Monaco, Lorenzo 33
Montughi 53
Museo Archeologico 41
Museo Stefano Bardini 23
Museo La Specola 27
Museo Salvatore Ferragamo 25
Museo Stibbert (Montughi) 53
Nardo di Cione 31
New Sacristy (Sagrestia Nuova) 36
Ognissanti 30, 32
Oltrarno 20
Opificio delle Pietre Dure 40
Orcagna, Andrea 15
Orsanmichele 15
Palazzo Medici-Riccardi 38
Piazza Santo Spirito 28
Piazzale Michelangelo 45
Pollaiolo, Antonio and Piero del 46
Ponte Vecchio 19
Pontormo, Jacopo 21, 22, 49, 51
Procession of the Magi (Gozzoli) 38
Refettorio della Chiesa di Ognissanti 30

Restaurants
  Antica Gelateria il David 17
  Bar Italia 52
  Beccofino 22
  Bella Ciao (Galluzzo) 52
  La Bianchina (Bottai) 52
  Buscioni 49
  Caffè Rivoire 16
  Cammillo 22
  Cantinetta Antinori 25
  Dolci e Dolcezza 44
  Il Latini 31
  Osteria Santo Spirito 28
  Trattoria Garga 31
  Trattoria Omero (Arcetri) 49
  Le Volpi e l'Uva 22
Robbia, Lucca della 46, 53
Roman Roads 14
Rossellino, Antonio 46
Sangallo, Giuliano da 48
San Lorenzo 35, 36, 37
San Marco 32
San Michele (Carmignano) 49
San Michele a San Salvi 32
San Miniato al Monte 45
Santa Croce 42
Santa Felicita 20
Santa Maria del Carmine 28
Santa Maria del Fiore 10
Santa Maria Novella 31
Santa Trinita 32
Second Cloister, Santa Croce 4
Settignano 53
Shops
  Castorina 24
  Madova 22
  Mercato Centrale 34
  N'uovo 30
  Peter Bazzanti and Son 24
  Romanelli 24
Società Canottieri (Circolo
  Canottieri) 20
Sotterraneo 37
Tabernacle 15
The Last Supper (Ghirlandaio) 30
Trinity (Masaccio) 31
Vasari, Giorgio 14, 17, 26

Villa Le Balze (Fiesole) 47
Villa Gamberaia (Settignano) 47, 54
Villa Medicea (Artimino) 48
Villa Medicea (Poggio a Caiano) 48
Villa Medicea della Petraia
(Castello) 47
Villa Medici (Fiesole) 47

VENICE

Accademia 115
Adoration of the Golden Calf
(Tintoretto) 70
Annunciations 63
Arsenale 91
Bacari 66
Badoer-Giustinian Chapel 90
Basilica di San Marco 107
Bellini, Gentile 115
Bellini, Giovanni 59, 75, 83, 100,
  110
Biblioteca Marciana (La Zecca) 103
Brodsky, Joseph 126
Buori, Giovanni 78
Burano 136
Caffè Corretto 99
Campiello del Pistor 65
Campo Santa Margherita 105, 108
Candi, Giovanni 98
Cannaregio 69
Canova, Antonio 59
Capella del Rosario 83
Capella di San Tarasio 88
Carpaccio, Vittore 88, 100, 117
Castello 78
Cima da Conegliano 70
Circolo Canottiere, see Socità
Canottiere
Coducci, Mauro 75, 78
Colleoni, Bartolomeo, monument 79
Conegliano, Cima da 70, 110
Corte del Duca Sforza 92
Doge's Palace (Palazzo Ducale) 101
Dorsoduro 104
Enchanted Evening 76
Excursion to the Venetian Lagoon
127

Fondazione Querini Stampalia 85
Food Shopping 69
Galleria Luce 94
Galleria Multigraphic 118
Gesuati 117
Gesuiti 74
Ghetto 70
Giudecca 122
Gloria di San Niccolò
(Montemezzano) 104
Guardi, Giovanni Antonio 104
Hotels
   Antica Locanda Montin 113
   Hotel Cipriani 123
   Hotel La Fenice et des Artistes 94
Istituto Universitaria di Architettura
di Venezia 58
Last Judgement (Tintoretto) 70
Last Judgement Mosaics (Torcello)
127
Lombardo, Pietro 77, 78, 83, 90
Lombardo, Tullio 75, 77, 78, 90
Longhena, Baldassare 117, 119
Madonna and Child Enthroned
(Negroponte) 90
Madonna and Child with Saints
(Tiepolo) 117
Madonna and Four Saints (Bellini)
87
Madonna della Misericordia
(Vivarini) 84
Madonna dell'Orto 70
Marble Gutters 102
Montemezzano, Francesco 104
Museo Archeologico 102
Museo Correr 100
Museo Fortuny 93
Negroponte, Antonio da 90
Palazzo Contarini del Bovolo 95
Palazzo Ducale, see Doge's Palace
Palladio, Andrea 90, 122, 126
Palma Vecchio 84
La Pietà 118
Raffaele Arcangelo 104
Il Redentore 122

Restaurants
   Acqua Pazza 94
   Al Covo 90
   Alla Madonna 68
   Alla Mascaron 84
   Alle Testiere 84
   American Bar 100
   Antica Locanda Montin 113
   Antico Capon 105
   Antico Dolo 67
   La Colonna 77
   Il Gelatone 76
   Da Ivo 98
   Didovich 78
   Do Mori 68
Fiaschetteria Toscana 75
   Harry's Bar 99
   La Pescheria Locanda Cipriani
(Torcello) 129
   Nico 114
   Osteria da Alberto 67
   Osteria Da Fiore 66
   Ristorante Al Covo 90
   Riviera 105
   Trattoria ai Cugnai 116
Rio Terrà dei Catecumeni 120
Roccatagliata, Niccolò 99
Saint Barbara Altarpiece 84
Saint George and the Dragon
(Carpaccio) 88
*Saint John the Baptist
   and Four Saints* (Conegliano) 70
San Francesco del Deserto 129
San Francesco della Vigna 90
San Giobbe 69
San Giorgio Maggiore 126
San Giovanni Crisostomo 75
San Lazzaro degli Armeni 130
San Marco, Basilica 101
San Michele 126
Santi Giovanni e PAOLO 79
San Moisè 99
San Nicolò dei Mendicoli 104
San Paolo & Santa Croce 58
San Salvatore 63

San Sebastiano 104
San Trovaso 114
San Zaccaria 87
San Zan Degolà 63
San Zanıpolo 79
Sansovino, Jacopo 74, 90, 103
Sant'Alvise 69
Sant'Apollonia 85
Santa Maria dei Miracoli 77
Santa Maria dell'Assunta (Torcello) 127
Santa Maria Formosa 84
Santa Maria Gloriosa dei Frari 59
Santa Maria dei Miracoli 77
Santa Maria della Salute 119
Save Venice Treasure Hunt 92
Scarpa, Carlo 58, 85
Scuola Grande dei Carmini 117
Scuola Grande di San Giovanni Evangelista 63
Scuola Grande di San Marco 78
Scuola Grande di San Rocco 62
Scuola Nuova Della Misericordia 74
Scuola di San Giorgio degli Schiavoni 88
Shops
  Colonna 78
  Domus 95
  Mascari 66
  Pastificio Giacomo Rizzo 76
  La Pescheria 105
  Rigattieri 93
  Tuttocasa 74
Storie di Tobiolo 104
Swimming Pools 123
Teatro Verde 126
The Miracle of the True Cross
  at the Bridge of San Lorenzo
(Bellini) 115
Tintoretto, Jacopo 62, 63, 70, 99, 120
Tomb of Alvise Diedo 83
Torcello 127
Traghetti 93

Venetian Islands 122
Veronese, Paolo 83, 104
Verrocchio, Andrea 79
Vivarini, Bartolomeo 59, 84
La Zecca, see La Biblioteca Marciana

ROBERT KAHN, creator and editor of the City Secrets series, is principal and founder of the award-winning firm Robert Kahn Architect, based in New York. A recipient of the Rome Prize in Architecture from the American Academy in Rome, he has received numerous awards from the New York chapter of the American Institute of Architects. His work has been featured in *The New York Times*, *The New York Times Magazine*, *Architectural Digest*, and *Metropolitan Home*, among other publications. He has taught design at Columbia University, Ohio State University, and Yale University, where he held a Davenport Chair Professorship.

THE AMERICAN ACADEMY IN ROME, a center for independent study and advanced research in the arts and humanities, is located on the Janiculum, the highest point within the walls of Rome. For the scores of artists, art historians, classicists, architects, and writers who have been awarded a Rome Prize, "the beauty and resources of the place, the quality and variety of the friendships, the depth of Rome, and the time and freedom to work" mark their stay there as among the top two or three experiences of a lifetime. Fellows, residents, visitors, and friends of the American Academy have generously shared their personal and professional insights in *City Secrets Florence & Venice*.

SAVE VENICE is an American nonprofit organization based in New York with an office in Venice and chapters in California and Boston. The mission of Save Venice is to preserve the art and architecture of Venice and to safeguard its cultural heritage by raising funds and providing educational programs. Founded in 1971, Save Venice has provided funding for the restoration of more than one hundred important works of art and buildings in Venice.

A portion of the proceeds from the sale of this book will be donated to the American Academy in Rome and Save Venice.

ACKNOWLEDGMENTS

I am deeply grateful to all the contributors who have so generously and eloquently shared their insights, expertise, and love of Florence and Venice. I extend my heartfelt thanks to the fellows, residents, and friends of the American Academy in Rome for sharing their remarkable depth of knowledge, as well as enthusiasm for this guide. The American Academy was the inspiration for this book, and I am profoundly grateful for the magical year I spent there. I would like to give generous thanks to those who helped bring this book to light: Adele Chatfield-Taylor, Sophie Consagra, Angela Hederman, Rae Hederman, Paul Pascal, Ingrid Bromberg Kennedy, and most especially my wife, Fiona Duff Kahn.

OTHER BOOKS FROM THE CITY SECRETS SERIES

CITY SECRETS ROME

"This idiosyncratic guide helps jaded visitors see the Eternal City anew."
—*The New York Times*

"Escape from the crowds and chaos can be a challenge in Rome, but help
comes in the form of *City Secrets Rome*."
—*Condé Nast Traveler*

CITY SECRETS LONDON

"Niles and Frasier Crane would love this book . . . crammed with tips
. . . Full marks for letting words do the work."
—*The Observer* (London)

"The next time I go to London, this book goes with me."
—*San Francisco Chronicle*

CITY SECRETS MANHATTAN

"In-the-know Big Apple-ites such as John Guare, Oliver Sacks, and Kate
Spade share their city secrets."
—*Vanity Fair*

"*City Secrets New York City*, is the latest installment in architect Robert
Kahn's invaluable series of insider guides for travelers."
—*New York Magazine*

CITY SECRETS MOVIES

"Surprising and revealing, *City Secrets Movies* is the instant response to the
lament 'There's nothing to watch.'"
—*Town & Country*

CITY SECRETS BOOKS

"So much concise and persuasive passion by such smart and interesting
people about so many intriguing and unfamiliar works! My next several
years are hereby, um, booked."
—Kurt Andersen, NPR radio host

*City Secrets books may be purchased at special quantity discounts
for business or promotional use. For information, please contact us at
info@fangduffkahn.com.*